EDUCATION AND THE
NATURE OF MAN

Other Books by the Same Authors

EARL C. KELLEY

EDUCATION FOR WHAT IS REAL

THE WORKSHOP WAY OF LEARNING

MARIE I. RASEY

THIS IS TEACHING

TOWARD MATURITY
(Hinds, Hayden and Eldredge)

EDUCATION
AND THE
NATURE OF MAN

BY EARL C. KELLEY
AND MARIE I. RASEY

Professors of Education
Wayne University

HARPER & BROTHERS, PUBLISHERS, NEW YORK

To The Memory of
JOHN DEWEY

CONTENTS

PREFACE

The authors of this book have worked together toward the improvement of their teaching methods for the past twelve years. It has been a mutually profitable and enriching association. Ideas which would not come clear for one often did for the other, and discussion of ways of applying ideas has been continuous. We have realized that we both have much to learn with regard to how people are motivated to action, under what conditions it is possible for the learner to release his energy for learning activity. We felt sure that no idea really matters until it has been put into action, and in our cases the action involved that most complicated of all creations, the human personality.

Education suffers from the fact that nearly everybody has ideas as to how school should be taught, but hardly anybody seems to have much basis in fact for his beliefs. These unsupported beliefs are held not only by the experts in education, but by parents, taxpayers, that man on the street. Teaching is the only profession concerning which Joe Doakes thinks he is an expert.

It occurred to us that a great deal has been learned in the first half of the twentieth century concerning the nature of the human organism—a vast amount as recently as the past ten years—and that it is not necessary any longer to have unsupported belief. The facts revealed from research now give us a basis for planning action for learning. We know enough now so that we can proceed more confidently in devising method than we have been able to do up to this time.

There are many teachers who are using methods which were devised in the early days of schools, long before anything was known about learning or about the organism to be taught. It is as though a present-day manufacturing plant were operating without knowledge of electricity.

This book is an attempt, then, to set forth some facts such as are to be had around the middle of the twentieth century, about the nature of the human organism as applicable to teaching and learning. It is an attempt to give people bases for their beliefs. In Part One we have tried to isolate some facts about people which seem to bear on human relations, or education in its best sense. In Part Two we discuss what seems to us to be the meaning of these facts. In Part Three we give some of the sources of our materials. Each part could have been much longer than it is. We think that, if the material is worthy, the less we burden our readers the more of them we will have. We think the book errs on the side of terseness and brevity.

The book is aimed primarily at attitudes and beliefs, because these are what control behavior. No teacher is going to teach differently until he believes differently, and can see himself in a new role. Any change which he may contemplate must seem reasonable to him.

You may be interested in our method of working. We did not make an outline and divide the chapters, with each author saying what he or she wanted to say in his own part. Every idea in the book was arrived at and agreed upon by both, so that the question as to who did the writing became of little consequence. None of the chapters could have been written by either author alone.

It will be revealed to those who read as far as Part Three that we have drawn upon many areas of learning. We have ranged over the fields of physics, chemistry, biology, psychology, sociology, psychiatry, anthropology. What is now known about human beings is scattered through many separate "disciplines."

We are indebted to many people for the ideas here expressed. We did not come by any of them by ourselves, operating in a social vacuum. Most of these benefactors are unknown to us, and therefore cannot be named. We have learned a great deal from our students in the Wayne University Education Workshop, both of us having been on its staff continuously since September, 1940. Here we were *forced* to experiment, because there were no known techniques on which to fall back.

We wish to express a special debt of gratitude to Dr. John Dewey for his assistance. During the months when the first draft was being prepared, we were in continuous correspondence with him. No one was more skilled in pin-pointing fallacies in some of our ideas. This has been an association which we will not forget.

Dr. Karen Horney made great contributions to our thinking during the period when we were preparing the manuscript. Both authors have sought her out, to test validity of ideas. We have always benefited, gained confidence, by these conferences.

Professor Adelbert Ames, Jr., of the Hanover Institute has helped us enormously. Through his experimentation in perception, he has furnished the missing building block which, we believe, makes our structure sound. We have long accepted the fact that one is literally built out of his experience, but it was not until we became acquainted with Professor Ames's work that we could see *how* this could be. Here we find scientific laboratory evidence which provides proof of the experimental point of view.

The authors gratefully acknowledge permission to quote from "John Brown's Body," in *Selected Works of Stephen Binet,* published by Rinehart and Company; and to Alfred Knopf, for permission to quote from *The Prophet,* by Kahlil Gibran; and from "Heaven," by Frank Townsend; and to the Frank Music Company, for two lines from "Orange-Colored Sky."

We wish also to express appreciation to Dr. J. W. Menge, Mrs. Mary Needham, and Mrs. Julia Baughman, who helped us, each in his or her own way.

E. C. K.
M. I. R.

February 16, 1952

PART ONE

CHAPTER 1

Introduction

A casual look at the social scene in the middle of the twentieth century reveals a situation which, in the long run, must be untenable for the human race. It would hardly be profitable to review all the symptoms. But the present mental state of most human beings who now inhabit the earth is not a happy one.

We see a general state of unrest, which inevitably results in conflict. We had hoped that the war would be over in 1945, but we have learned to our dismay that it has only been transferred and diffused. Where formerly we knew whom we were fighting, and where he was, now our enemies are among us, and we can scarcely tell friend from foe. Nation is arráyed against nation, group against group, neighbor against neighbor.

This results in a state of general apprehension. Fear and hatred are abroad in the world, and probably no human being anywhere who is alert enough to take in his surroundings is free from them. (1)*

Life was not always that way. Only a half century ago, people lived in comparative tranquillity. It is true that labor was long, pay was small, and acquisition of world's goods—a higher standard of living—was difficult. But man, most places on the earth, could reasonably expect to live out the years of his life and to die in peace, surrounded by those whom he had created. Now every informed person on the earth knows that he can be destroyed from afar, by means so staggering that within himself he has no way with which to cope with them. He only half expects to die a natural death.

*Numbers in parentheses throughout the text refer to sources given in Part Three.

3

The disappearance of tranquillity is perhaps the most salient symptom of our time. The accompanying anxiety results in such sociological symptoms as a shifting population, disintegration of the home, with the mounting divorce rate, juvenile delinquency, adult crime, and so on.

It seems apparent that a certain amount of tranquillity and a certain amount of reasonable expectation is essential to the well-being of humankind. If man stays in a continued state of anxiety, he will develop abnormalities in varying degree. That is why the present condition of man is untenable, and this implies that he will have to find ways of coming to grips with the causes of his instability.

This period of apprehension and unrest can be considered as temporary. Man has, throughout his history, been called upon from time to time to make major and difficult adjustments to new situations. He has repeatedly worked himself out of times of trouble. He has always worked toward getting himself out of untenable relationships with his environment, and into tenable ones. Thus has his sanity been maintained. Man's progress has been a succession of untenable situations which have called for contriving solutions. These, in turn, have led to creative effort bringing about new difficulties.

The inevitable period of quiet that follows a time of trouble has not been an end, but rather an opportunity for refreshment, the better to meet oncoming dilemmas. What is new in the present situation is that, whereas in the past man could wait for the situation to right itself, we now have to face the fact that the world may be destroyed while we wait. This fact gives urgency to our present time, unlike any we have known before. (2)

When the first living creature emerged from water and became a land animal, it faced a whole new set of problems. From some such creature, man has evidently evolved. In doing so, he had to cope with the difficulties of the land, but he achieved new freedom. The confining aspects of life in water no longer appealed to him because he valued the new freedom above the cost of it. So well did he take to the land that he abandoned gills altogether, and now cannot endure water for more than a few minutes. He had to come to grips with new methods of travel, with differing temperatures and altitudes. His body had to invent a method of temperature control which is a marvel to contemplate. (3)

Long after adjustments were made to a world of air, man was forced by his own creativeness to come to grips with the problem of using fire. The learning of the uses of fire called for a whole new set of responses. He could then regulate, to a degree, the temperatures that surrounded him. He could produce new food for himself, and use many kinds of food which had formerly been of no value to him. He could live in a much wider variety of places. He could make tools which enabled him to cope with his environment better than before. He achieved new freedoms in many ways, and likewise he had new responsibilities thrust upon him. (4)

Early man, filled with awe in contemplation of the universe, sought help outside himself in his fight for life. He invented gods, and placed his faith in them, because they were stronger than he. He invented a separate god for each need, and soon he had so many gods that the appeasement of all of them consumed most of his time and energy. He became a slave to his own invention, and fear of supernatural consequences filled his mind. A great release and a new life came to him when he became monotheistic. Then he had only one god to appease, and this change resulted in large new freedoms.

In more recent times, man's relationships and consequent outlooks have been modified in other ways. The work of Galileo called for a new orientation to man's universe. Whereas man's thinking and attention, at least in the Western world, had up to this time been earthbound, he now reached out to an expanding universe, and he became a creature not of the earth alone but of a whole galaxy of worlds. While it is true that man had always been interested in the heavens, Galileo introduced the disturbing idea of the possibility of other worlds, which might share the interests of the Deity. Galileo marked really the beginning of experimental science. At the same time, Kepler gave new ideas about analysis and quantitative measurements, so that man was able to take his problems apart and reckon them. This at least gave him a new approach. By making the error of assuming that the whole was the sum of its parts, Kepler probably created an habitual approach which, useful as it was, no longer serves. Even though man now needs to abandon this notion, certainly analysis and quantitative measurements have long dominated his ways of dealing with his environment, and doubtless gave him added freedoms over what he had known before. The work of Galileo and Kepler at least caused men to make a new adjustment and to form new habits of dealing with the problems of life. (5)

The present period of transition, the present untenable situation, is brought about by the great increase in the supply and use of energy. Man's material progress has been a matter of finding new usable energy outside himself. This knowledge came to him in a small way when he learned to heat his dwelling and to cook his food with fire. He got an added boost when he succeeded in domesticating animals to do work for him. But the process of capturing outside energy from there on was slow. In fact, up to the time of the invention of the steam engine, no man had more power than that of his own muscles and those of his animals, except a small use of wind and water, and no man could travel faster than his animals could go. Long after the invention of the steam engine, most men knew no addition of energy. Farming, even into this century, made no use of energy beyond that supplied by men, oxen, and horses. Abraham Lincoln was the first commander in chief who could get to his troops faster than any other man through the ages had been able to. He could move about at the speed of thirty-five miles per hour, but George Washington could move no faster than Julius Caesar.

The vast production of energy, starting slowly with the steam engine and culminating (so far) in atomic energy, has produced a change in the conditions under which man lives that is as great, perhaps, as the change made when the first creature emerged from the water to land. These great changes, it would seem, must always result in great general anxiety, because they call for departure from the known, and no one knows how the unknown will work out. The emerging land creature which was to become man may have suffered great anxiety, and it certainly would have done so had it had experience with which to appraise its real situation. Man is informed enough now to know that this new evolvement, while holding great potentialities for his betterment and a whole set of new freedoms, also carries the likely prospect of his complete undoing. He is again in danger of becoming a slave to his own invention, or perhaps even of being destroyed by it.

Virtually unlimited energy has worked many changes in the world in which man now lives. He is no longer earthbound. For millions of years he has been sure of one thing and that is that he must move over the surface of the earth, which takes time. Now he must accustom himself to the fact that he can go through the air at great speed, and that he can also go under the water. Enemies he has always had, but they had to move over the surface of the earth, and they had to come to him at a pace limited by that fact. Missiles had to be thrown along the surface of the earth, and there was safety to be found behind obstacles. Now the enemy can be so far above him that he cannot even hear him, so that missiles dropped by the enemy can come utterly unheralded, and from what was formerly an impossible direction. Indeed, the missiles can come from above without the enemy actually being there at all. If the hurling of missiles is inadequate for man's destruction, the enemy himself can float down from the stratosphere, and not make his approach in the accustomed way. A view over a broad expanse of water, with nothing but limitless waves in sight, formerly meant a peaceful scene. But now the enemy may be lurking just beneath those waves, carrying weapons more deadly than were ever before known, and the scene may not be peaceful at all.

Great extension of the use of energy has thrown man's time-honored notions of his location out of line. Very recently in man's history his rate of travel was slow, and he knew just about what was involved in getting from one place to another. Now he can move so rapidly that what he formerly used as a basis of location no longer suffices. The fact is that it is no longer necessary even to move the physical body from place to place in order to be there. We no longer have to go to the ball park in order to attend a baseball game. We can both see and hear what is going on simply by pushing some buttons. It is commonplace for us, in the same manner, to "be" in Australia, Moscow, and Rio all within a fifteen-minute span. We can know what is going on in Indonesia and London at virtually the same time. This new power yields an enormous increase in new freedom, but it carries such responsibility that man cannot be complacent when he faces it.

The new vast production of energy has upset, and probably will completely destroy, man's system for sharing the world's goods. The method of distribution of the goods of earth has for long been based on the sweat of the brow. Work has become a great virtue; we even hold a moral attitude toward it. During the economic difficulties of the 1930's we had people raking leaves where there were no leaves, and shoveling snow that did not exist, because we believed that a man was damaged when he got something for which he had not made a corresponding effort.

We are not here interested in the validity of this moral concept. But the machine has already taken over much of the work of the world, and promises, in the quite near future, to take most of the rest of it. It is said that it is now possible to make, synthetically, a complete suit of men's clothes better than is now known, without benefit of tailors, weavers, or sheepherders. What will happen when impersonal energy takes over the work of the world, and the brow has nothing to sweat about? Man will have to work out other criteria for distributing the goods of earth. He has already displayed anxiety in this area, and has tried to meet the dilemma by slowing down the production of new machines, by demanding "stand-by" personnel, and so on. Man sees his area of usefulness, the world's need of him, gradually disappearing, and he does not like it nor is he prepared for it.

This condition may be the completion of some sort of cycle. When man invented his gods he needed them to be greater than he, so that he could depend upon them for help. So he made them all-knowing, all-powerful, and ever-present. Now man approaches these attributes himself. He can do all the things that formerly were attributed to magic. He can fly through the air with the greatest of ease. He can be anywhere he wants to be in such a short time that time is scarcely a factor. He can know what is going on almost anywhere without the passage of time, and without going to the place in person. Achieving these powers has not brought security. There is need for new concepts of his own potencies, and of ways to use them to meet his new contingencies.

It is easy to see that man has developed, through long use, a set of patterns which no longer serve him. When they were created they served him well, but in the light of new conditions they have outlived their usefulness. In order to meet entirely new conditions he will need a new set of patterns. These patterns will enable him to make use of his new freedoms. This he can achieve, because he has always derived his patterns of living by making adjustments to his externality. He has dealt with the conditions around him as he perceived them. This he must and, if given time, doubtless will do again. It is the bridge over which he formerly passed and can pass again, to a way of life which will be tenable and more free from anxiety than the one he now knows.

Something new has been added, in the same sense as is so aptly illustrated by Ouspensky in his illustration of the cone sitting on the transparent table. If the cone is viewed from below, it appears as a circle. It can only be considered as two-dimensional, and can only be thought of as a circle, a surface. There is nothing else with which to think about it. But if the observer comes out from under the table and views it from above, a new dimension is added and wholly new ways of thinking about it are imperative.

We need a new concept of time. Time has meaning in considering how long it takes to move from one place to another. This notion has never been too valid, as we have all had the experience of time seeming to stand still in crisis. People who have been in automobile accidents often report long stretches of time between events which must have been almost simultaneous. Earlier reference has been made to the fact that Lincoln was the first commander in chief who could go to war areas faster than Caesar, but geographically his war was puny compared to others to follow. Franklin Roosevelt could visit various areas of a world conflict so quickly that the actual time consumed was almost negligible. We can practically be everywhere simultaneously, and we need to learn how to think of time in some other way than that to which we are accustomed.

We need a new concept of distance. This is so closely related to the new concept of time that it may be hard to see it separately. We are used to thinking of some things as close by, others as far away. The faraway ones have been of little concern to us, and living in that framework, if we could keep the unpleasant items of life far away and the pleasant ones nearby, it gave us a method of operating. But now we have to get used to the fact that nothing on earth is really far away.

We have long met unsatisfactory conditions by flight or fight. But now neither flight nor fight has any significance. If we flee from our troubles we have no place to flee to, because there is no place that is far away. If we stay to fight we find ourselves up against power far greater than our own, so that we have small chance of making this reaction successful. The fact that nothing is far away then cuts into our most basic method of meeting adversity.

We need a new concept of philosophy. It is in philosophy that we project beyond our present condition toward better ways of acting. Philosophy is the growing edge of creativity, since change (improvement) cannot come to be until it has been projected. The need for philosophers, and the attainment of workable personal philosophies, has never been greater.

The role of the philosopher is to take all present available data, especially from science, and speculate from there, on its meaning for human life; to project as well as can be from the data. The early philosophers had little data, and thus should have been less accurate in their speculations than should be possible now.

Our modern philosophers have adopted rules to which they adhere, somewhat in disregard of present knowings. A good example is some of the mental gymnastics in which they indulge in the realm of logic. They also depend too much on the historical approach. Therefore, what they produce is static, since the rules and the history are static.

We need philosophers who are aware of the flowing and becoming nature of life and of the universe; who see that we are all like Eliza crossing the river; and who will help us plan and project from that notion. This calls for the abandonment of their static ideas, and a reaching out for that which may be useful in action. The role of the philosopher is to argue beyond the data, not behind it or in disregard of it.

We need a new concept of our personal relationships to other human beings. The fact that every human being on the earth is near, is indeed our neighbor, calls for new ways of thinking about the other peoples of the earth, whom for so long we have held to be no concern of ours. (6) In the past distance has been one of the basic factors in human relations. We considered that those who lived on other parts of the earth were held out of our lives and therefore did not concern us. If people annoyed us too much, we moved out beyond the frontier, where other people could not reach us. When it was not possible to move away from people we found ways of building walls around ourselves so that others, although physically present, were not able to intrude. Thus we found flight possible without actually moving the body away. These walls were much like the ones we built in the form of forts, in order to keep enemies away, because they had only one plane of access to us. The personal walls of exclusion that we have habitually built around us are now no more tenable than the forts of old. Since nobody is far, man's chief task in life is in adjustment to others. There is now no escape from this necessity, and one's success or failure in life depends largely upon this adjustment. That there are other people in our externality who impinge upon us and upon whom we impinge is one of the basic facts of life.

Because of this mutual impingement, we are shaped and made by the other personalities around us. Just as the shape of a crystal is determined in part by the burgeoning of other crystals, just as the cell in the honeycomb is six-sided because of the other cells, so the human conformation is determined by the presence and pressure of other human beings. We, therefore, in this new world without time or distance must abandon our characteristic habits of personal isolation, and devise new patterns for meeting our fellows. We must arrive at ways of living which will make human association part of our own development and enable us to gain stimulation from association. We must learn how to make an asset out of the necessity brought about by the destruction of our opportunity to isolate ourselves.

Our habitual notion of exclusion is shown in the way we seek to establish boundaries of one sort or another. International boundaries, for example, were established, for the most part, along lines which we thought we could defend, so that we might exclude enemies and other peoples we held to be undesirable. These boundaries were usually physical barriers—rivers, oceans, or mountains. They have now lost all real significance, because no enemy would bother to cross them on the surface of the earth. They really do not exist, but we continue to act as though they did. We talk of sovereignty, which means absolute control over a certain piece of territory, and the right to do just as we please up to that boundary. Of course we have no such right because what we now do affects all other human beings on the earth.

We build boundaries in our communities, between members of various churches, and between members of creeds and races. It is an effort to strengthen the untenable walls around ourselves. It is an attempt to continue to deny the fact that all mankind is together, and belongs together. It is a valiant pretense based on a denial of the obvious facts.

We need to face the future instead of the past. We have long habituated ourselves to holding to the past and trying to make the future as much like the past as we could. This attempt is probably to be expected, since we are apt to have more confidence in the known than in the unknown. It seems we even idealize the past, remembering best that which was pleasant and blocking out of our minds that which was unpleasant. This habit of remembering is a great boon to action. If we recalled only our failures we would hesitate to act. The past thus comes to appear much more desirable than it really was. We have sought after truths which would be reliable for all time and have clung to what seemed to be absolutes. We hoped for something on which we could firmly place our feet in order to face whatever storms we might encounter. Because change came slowly until recently, and because individual lives are short, it has seemed at times that certain truths were eternal. The shifting was slow enough to serve the short span of the individual, and the next generation had its own set of "eternal" truths, somewhat different.

The great increase of energy has stepped up the tempo of life so that none of these verities will now last out an ordinary lifetime. We cannot prepare for a changing world in specifics because the specifics are not given. The planning, or lack of it, of our large cities shows our lack of ability to see specific needs even for a few years ahead. Where recently we needed only hitching posts, we now need landing fields. The failure to prepare for specifics is brought forcibly to the attention of anyone who has to make his

way from an airport to a downtown hotel. Often the total saving of
time gained by the speed of the airplane is lost through the lack of
foresight in the building of the city. We, therefore, have to prepare
for the unknown by the adoption of attitudes which will enable us
to expect and welcome the new and novel. In this attitude toward
the future we can find security to meet it, whatever it may bring.
For our static attitudes toward life we can substitute outlooks
which will take into account the evolving and becoming nature of
life. (7)

We need a new concept of wholeness. In the past, when we have
made an approach to any problem, our first impulse has been to
take it apart, so that we could see it better. We *were* able to see the
parts better, but this did not enable us to see the whole. This is
such a common practice that we are unskilled in synthesis, most
skilled in analysis. We come to see now that we never find out what
the whole is like by looking at its parts. Part examination has led to
abstraction, based on a sort of reconstruction which does not bring
back the entity we started with. We need to come to learn that the
whole is not the sum of its parts, but more, because it has an entity
of its own. This entity is destroyed by analysis, revealed by synthesis. We need to be alert to the dangers of statistics, recognizing
them for what they can teach, but alert to their fallacies and
weaknesses.

We need a new concept of freedom. Throughout this chapter it
has appeared again and again that new conditions bring new freedoms. The beasts of the jungle have freedom of a sort. It is freedom
to do as they please as long as they are strong enough and swift
enough to do it. But the limitations of their kind of living are
apparent. Man's progress toward civilization has been a series of
abandonments of freedom, to take on others.

When the creature that was to become man emerged from water
he had to develop a new concept of freedom. He gave up one sort
of security, to seek another. There were all kinds of things he could
do which he had not been able to do before. But the new freedoms
brought new hazards and new responsibilities.

The emergence of unlimited energy has brought man another
whole new set of freedoms to which he must accustom himself.
Fast transportation, made possible by harnessing energy, has made

it possible for him to live in better places and still do his work. He can spread himself out much more than formerly. Some people commute between New York and Chicago, working in both places.

Perhaps the greatest development of freedom is that which comes from freedom from drudgery. It has been commonplace in the history of men for many of them to live in actual slavery. When the slavery has been removed, the struggle for existence has been such that not much addition of freedom was achieved. It did not matter much whether man bent his back at the crack of the slave driver's whip or from hard economic necessity. Now it seems likely that so much of the work of the world will be done by energy outside himself that man will not need to submit to economic slavery. He will have time on his hands and freedom to use it. He will need a new concept of the use of this freedom.

In another sense, the progress of freedom has been a social and ethical one. When there were few of him on the earth, man could seek solitude, so that he might do just as he pleased. He can no longer do this, so that he is limited in his ability to do as he pleases. But by association with others he can do more things than he could do before, and can achieve more time to do them. When the full impact of the importance of the social good dawns upon man he will see that his greatest freedom lies in achieving freedom for all. This new concept will then be a far cry from the original one of the right to do as he pleases, but it will bring him time, energy, and method for achieving creative action never known before. He will then be free to spend himself as he needs to, not as he is forced to by circumstances which he could not control. When man comes to be able to spend himself as he sees fit within his social framework he will then have achieved the ultimate in civilized freedom.

The establishment of patterns which will meet the needs of the times will have to be facilitated beyond the natural course of living. Events are rushing headlong, and because of the immense potential for destruction in our new release of energy, more rapid adjustment is demanded. The way by which man has facilitated and must facilitate his adjustment is through education.

Education is the way by which the past is made available to the individual more rapidly than would ordinarily be the case. Through education it becomes unnecessary for each individual to repeat the entire history of his race. It is here that man differs from the beasts. A cat can learn certain ways of living, but the cats of today are no farther along than cats have ever been. They cannot facilitate their evolvement.

While knowledge remains subjective, experiences which acquaint the young with the developments to date give them an advantage over those who have gone before. By using the educative process, it is possible that man may short-cut the slow process of adjustment. This short-cut will call for an education which uses the past, but brings a critical attitude toward the past and does not depend upon it except where it serves. Such education calls for the use of that which is usable and the rejection of that which does not serve. It will avoid the veneration of the past, but will recognize the progress that has been made. It will hold that knowledge is not power until it can be brought to bear upon the solution of the problems of the future. It will work toward the development of a critical, skeptical, and alert man, who has respect for his own thinking, who will want to direct his own actions, and who will expect to take the responsibility for his own mistakes.

This book, then, will be devoted to ways in which education can be brought into line with the actual situation that confronts man, and with his adjustment to that situation. In Part I we shall set forth a number of facts about man and his externality. These facts are not now in the realm of opinion, or at least not entirely so. Each fact specified is as near truth as it is possible to come at the present time, and is based largely on laboratory evidence. Some of them may seem so commonly known that they hardly need to be stated, but all of them, we believe, bear directly on the problems of education and of living, and all need to be presented. This book is an attempt to bring educational practices into line with the demands of the present and the foreseeable future, by means of what is now known about the human organism in its social and material setting.

CHAPTER 2

The Dynamic of Change

Creation of the Earth as part of the universe and including mankind is a process now going on, not an event of the past. So it is with the life of the individual. Those who join in and help with the process of creation are "good" and live in harmony with God in whatever image they see Him; those who seek to stem the tide of creation or to exert force contrary to it are the evil ones. They cry "Halt! I like it this way"; they proudly call themselves conservatives and sing dismally of the Rock of Ages. Failure to continue the process of creation, or diverting it beyond the lines of its own force brings perversion, misery, degradation, violence, and untimely death. Man's orderly progress toward cooperation has been constantly retarded by the beneficiaries of the status quo through emphasis upon selfishness, group egotism, nationalism, regional pride! We face the wages of their sin.

—Howard Lane

Change is the basic phenomenon of the universe. To help us to cope with the problems confronting us in our effort to adjust to a new world so very different from the old, we have some knowledge which will serve. Man has been busy inquiring into his own nature and that of the universe in which he must survive or perish. Most of these knowings have been arrived at in laboratories; some of them have been inferred from other discoveries. They range over many fields—medicine, physiology, psychology, psychiatry, sociology, anthropology, physics, chemistry, biology, astronomy. They all bear upon man and his environment, and hence are apropos to the problem of human adjustment.

It is our purpose to set forth some rather fundamental findings in order that we may relate the problems of education to them. Since all knowledge is tentative, these findings are tentative. They are the best we know at this time, and our decisions and actions must be based upon them. This is what man has always done: based his actions upon what seemed to be the facts at the time when action was demanded. His error has been in that he did not regard his facts as tentative, and when his actions went wrong he was at a loss to know the reasons. He was also often misled in believing that items which changed slowly did not change at all.

Nothing in the organic or the inorganic world remains the same as it was. There is only one thing we know for certain about tomorrow or next year, and that is that it will be different from today or from this year. If there is one thing written on this temporary paper which we feel sure will be true a hundred years from now, it is this fact. (8)

How can we have one fact which will stand while the others are modified by new exploration and new learning? Perhaps it is because this is not a fact at all in the sense that we usually think of facts. A fact implies permanence, something we can tie to. It may be that the concept of change as a universal law is the denial of fact rather than a fact itself. It is a recognition of impermanence, a statement of fundamental process or movement rather than a fundamental fact. We may be merely having word trouble when we refer to a process as a fact, and a redefinition of our terms might help us to arrive at meaning. Since change is everywhere, everything is process.

That change is universal seems so obvious and observable that it is hardly worth writing about. But while almost anyone would concede this observation to be true, most human beings act as though it were not true. We try too hard to find something on which to stand, on which to seek permanence. We feel that we need a base—a solid footing from which to take the next step. So we seek after things and values which will not change, so that we may stand upon them. It is not enough for us to verbalize the phenomenon of change. We must learn to live with it, and to act as though we believe it. As in many another instance, our actions reveal our real beliefs, regardless of the protestations of our lips.

It may be that the reason we are so habituated to seek changelessness is because, before the invention of energy outside ourselves, the tempo of change in some things was much slower. Man's span of life is short enough so that, in that slow tempo, there appeared to be a great deal more permanence than now exists anywhere. Because change was rather imperceptible within man's span of life, he mistook it for stability. One of the causes of his present anxiety is that he can no longer make this assumption.

When we get the concept of change into our organisms so that we act as though it was so, we will not try to plan for eternity. This is the very point where we make the error set forth by Howard Mumford Jones when he says that the school curriculum is always planned for eternity instead of for time. It is not just in planning school programs that we do this. It permeates our whole lives.

At the risk of laboring the obvious, let us examine the evidence for believing that change is universal.

The simplest evidence lies in what the casual observer can see with his own eyes. Nothing that we can think of from our youth really abides in the same way that it existed at that time. Our mode of living, the things we knew and cherished, the people we thought we would know and love forever, all are gone or modified so that their meanings have changed. This is why the old man who retires and wants to have one more look at the scene of his childhood is so often disappointed. He finds some things which seem remotely familiar, but most are new or do not fit. He looks around, a sickly smile that discloses disappointment appears on his face, and he goes back to the life he presently knows, saddened by the knowledge that what he thought was there waiting for him, ready again to support him, no longer exists. What he has for support is to be found in the place where he has spent the last few years. (9)

This point is well illustrated in the experience of the son of a pioneer family who replaced his father's old log house with a fine modern one. He included in the new house, however, a fireplace equipped with a tin reflector such as his mother had used to bake biscuits in his boyhood. When all was complete he asked his aged Quaker mother to bake biscuits for him. This she did, and as she placed them, golden brown, before him, she said, "Now, Pliny, if thee had thy boy's appetite—"

Our knowledge of the nature of matter and its atomic and molecular make-up tells us that matter lacks permanence. We are used to the idea that the water flowing down the side of the mountain is on its way to the sea. We know, however, that the rocks in the mountain are just as surely on their way to the sea. It is only a matter of time. The failure to comprehend the time element causes us to assume a difference in kind, instead of a difference in speed, of change.

The desk on which I write seems permanent. I have known it for about twenty years and it looks substantially the same to me now as it did when it was new. But we would all be surprised if it should survive a thousand years. The desk is going through the same process of deterioration as a cantaloupe. The cantaloupe simply does it faster, and gets back to the elements sooner. The cantaloupe seems equally slow about this return when compared to U238, which will scarcely behave for us at all.

The physical or inanimate world is endless in its examples of this point. Scientists have carried us far beyond our own small world and our brief flicker of time. The astronomers are pushing our knowledge of the universe farther and farther, finding the whole structure in process of change. They speak of old stars and new stars, telling us of the difference in chemical composition between them. They tell us that our own sun is spending itself and will sometime be cold, providing it does not explode as other suns have. They are not surprised to look out into the far reaches and find that a star they knew has exploded and is in process of rapid disintegration.

We have seen growth and death in the plant and animal worlds, and are well accustomed to them. We are familiar with the life cycles of both our plants and our animals, so that we do not expect a tomato plant to go on year after year, or our cats, dogs, or horses to outlive us. We may not be so well aware of the impermanence of our own bodies.

We are composed of active cells made of active molecules. These cells are constantly being nurtured from the outside, and continuously being modified by that nurture as the nurture is modified. New cells are forming; old cells are dying, and their remains are being carried away and eliminated. When you meet an old friend whom you have not seen for ten or twenty years you may exclaim that he hasn't changed a bit. The fact is that there are very few cells of him that were with him when you saw him last. In a physical sense, he is an almost entirely new organism which you have never seen before. (10)

Bodily changes and attitude changes are so closely related that it is not possible to separate them. If for some reason your body shoots an excess charge of adrenalin into your blood stream, what you are in terms of what you do becomes different. This is partly the reason why the old friend mentioned above may look just the same to you, but you find that it is not possible to discover anything to talk to him about. You say, rather glibly, that his interests and yours have grown apart. Rather sadly we must admit that you and he are really different organisms. The reminiscing on the lives you once led together and hold in common memory soon runs out, and then two new persons face each other needing either to part or to build new mutual interests.

It is complicating enough to realize that the human organism in its totality and all that it encounters is in flux. Life is further complicated by the fact that there is constant change in relatedness. And our relatedness to our environment, other people, and things is the basis for our orientation. We live in a milieu of movement, and what we are and can do depends upon how we can relate ourselves to a world of movement. Since we cannot pin things and people down, we need to become accustomed to a world of movement and changing relatedness, as well as to the idea of change in itself. (11)

Some hold that the organism itself is so constituted that change is essential to it. This is a thought contrary to the notion that if we could only get something to tie to we would be able to achieve security. The artists and the architects are becoming aware of this need. The masterpieces survive because they somehow escape monotony. Dorner's ideas on space in art, as well as Gropius' direct statement of this idea, help to establish the recognition of this need.

Life, then, really means process, movement, flux. We never really arrive. We never become, but are always in process of becoming. We are in a stream, where action is demanded for survival. If life is itself process, if change and movement are the basic phenomena, then we need to take a new look at what we have been pleased to call fact and foundation.

All these conclusions will have to be repeated until people stop acting as though they were not so. When human beings are able to get control of the reality of process and movement, they will stop seeking their security in the unchanging and begin to live in a changing world, where their security actually lies.

CHAPTER 3

Man's Structure and Method

And then came man.
But long before
There had been slime,
With sun upon it,
Till it lived and moved.
It had its being.
Thus
Up from the sea,
Up toward the sun
By multiple becomingness
Man came to be.
— Marie I. Rasey

We see, then, that the organism called man is part of a changing
world. He moves in a process of which he must partake and with
which he must cope. He is in and of a universe which has movement and change as its basic characteristic.

The remainder of Part I isolates some of the characteristics
of the human organism which seem at this time to be true. These
characteristics are at least some which have to be taken into account when we plan to educate the organism. Conversely, any
method, practice, or habit of educating which is at variance with or
contradicts these characteristics will fail of its purpose.

1. MAN IS A UNIT OF ENERGY SEEKING TO SPEND ITSELF

Since man is in and of nature, we can get some clues as to what
he is like from the nature of the universe itself. We are coming to
appreciate the fact that all matter is energy. We know from the
structure of the atom that this is true. Even in the most stable forms

—wood, rocks, earth—we know that the basic element is the atom, and that the atom is not a solid particle but an organization in which energy is locked.

Thus perishes another of the persistent dualities—that of matter and energy. There is no such duality—no such separation. Nonliving matter is in the process of deterioration or of expenditure. The rates of expenditure vary greatly, but the process is the same. The wood out of which this desk is made is in a slow process of exchange, and so will continue if conditions remain the same. But if the house in which the desk stands should burn, the conditions would be changed, and the process of return to the elements of which the desk is made would be greatly speeded up. Fire is a rapid method of change but not nearly so rapid as atomic fission. In this newly discovered method, it has become possible to release all the energy that constitutes the matter involved within a space of time so short that to us it is instantaneous.

The human organism, being composed of atoms, is therefore an embodiment of energy, and energy is always seeking to spend itself as it can. This expenditure is rapid in some cases, slow in others. A recent article in a popular magazine tells that a man weighing two hundred pounds would be a speck just visible with a magnifying glass if all the interatomic space were taken out and nothing remained except the neutrons, protons, and electrons. What he really is, then, is a bulk of space, or an embodiment of energy. (12)

The problem of understanding this phenomenon is complicated by the fact that the human organism has some control over the expenditure of the energy of which it is constituted. This does not appear to be true of rock or wood. In these the expenditure depends solely upon the characteristics of the atoms and of the surrounding conditions. The ability to choose is a characteristic of living things, and more especially of man.

How will the energy be spent, since there is a possibility of choice? How will it be conserved in some cases, burned rapidly in others, as seems to fit the need of the organism? How may the dynamics of stored energy be controlled and released to the advancement of the organism? These are questions which confront those of us who would educate.

2. ALL LIVING ORGANISMS, INCLUDING MAN, POSSESS THE DYNAMIC OF GROWTH

This seems to be a continuously operating dynamic, throughout the lives of all living organisms. It seems to be at least one of the salient differences between the dead and the living, the animate and the inanimate. We are aware that we are using another dualism; it may be that in time this dualism will disappear. There are respectable scientists today who say that there is no difference in kind between the animate and the inanimate, but only a difference in degree. When more scales fall from our eyes we may see that too. Other equally respectable scientists see a basic difference between the living cell, particularly those cells which procreate, and the structure of a rock. One is in the process of going from order of a sort to disorder. The other is in process of making order out of disorder. At the present moment we find it easier to go along with the latter, since we do behold a phenomenon which needs some explanation.

The individual is at first a one-celled creature built from sperm and ovum. It has a unique atomic structure, practically impossible to duplicate, but it does not remain a one-celled structure. Something within it causes it to become many celled, and to grow in the direction laid down by its atomic structure. Thus the egg-sperm (zygote) of the cat does not grow to be a man, that of the grape does not become an oak. Catness and grapeness are there in the beginning of the individual.

This dynamic of growth seems to be an ability to take out of surroundings, food, air, liquids, that which the organism can use to build more of itself. Since the structure is an embodiment of energy, this is the ability to convert energy held in one form into another. When we say that the human organism is an embodiment of energy we need to account for the source of that energy. We cannot say that it was all there in egg and sperm, because they are one cell. So the energy of which we are built has to be continuously converted from the surrounding media. This building through conversion is growth, and the force or purpose that causes it to happen is its dynamic. This dynamic is at the center of life itself.

Growth will not always and necessarily take place. Conditions have to be propitious. When conditions are not propitious, growth is arrested. When growth is arrested too long, death ensues. Growth, then, is more or less continuous at accelerated or decelerated rates as long as life lasts. The permanent cessation of growth is death, and at this point the structure that was the purposing human being takes on the disintegrating characteristics of the inanimate. How growth can be encouraged and directed becomes the answer to the question as to how life may be best lived.

3. Man Is Able to Direct His Own Evolvement

Growth, then, is the dynamic of all living things, from the simplest to the highest forms. It is essentially the capacity and demand to take energy in the form of the environing media and to convert or transfer it, making it part of the organism itself. No living thing can maintain its state of being alive without this power or capacity.

All lower creatures do this without conscious effort or understanding. They are completely the victims of circumstances. If the living cell is fortunate enough to fall into circumstances which are propitious, it will survive and thrive. Some of the growths attained, especially by plants, in unusually good conditions are tremendous. If, however, seed falls upon rocks, or if the egg is deposited in the wrong kind of water, the organism has no choice, and so must perish. Plants have met this risk by being prodigal in the production of spore or seed, so that only one in many need find suitable surroundings in order for the species to survive.

The human organism is not similarly helpless. It has mobility not possessed by most plants and some animals. It is able to seek suitable media.

In addition to this ability to move, it has a highly developed nervous system which gives it certain capacities not possessed by other creatures even when they are mobile. These capacities come from the evolvement of brain cortex and from the other accompaniments of the efficient nervous equipment.

Through this development man, better than any other creature, can remember and foresee. The ability to foresee is based on the ability to remember. He can thus know how one set of circumstances worked for him, and to imagine what conditions he may find desirable. Until he was able to remember and to foresee, his mobility could be used only in a haphazard manner. (13)

This enables man to control or create his own circumstances, at least to a degree. There are still many conditions which he has not been able to control completely, but he can do much more about them than he could before he developed his present cortex. He has made great strides in this direction since he discovered how to produce great quantities of energy outside himself. The weather is an example of an outside circumstance which has had much to do with man's nurture. While he has not been able actually to affect the weather much, he has invented many ways of living with it, which amount to the modification of its effects. We still have hot days, but many men now spend them in air-conditioned places, so that their actual weather is cool. Man has dammed up the waters of the rivers, so that he is no longer completely dependent upon rain. It may be within his grasp soon to modify the weather itself. There is some question as to whether this ability will increase or decrease his anxiety. It will be one more item of adjustment, like the alterations in time and space.

A great step in evolvement comes as man increasingly learns how to make his circumstances before they have a chance to make him. He can be what he wills to be if he can control his surrounding media, for out of that he is made. (14)

Some of the lower animals seem to have the dawn of this ability, but it is not advanced to the point where it effectively serves. We often mistake that which has been built into the lower organisms as reflex or instinct for reasoning power. The squirrel buries nuts, and we say he foresees the winter, but he sometimes buries nuts in the spring, if he comes into possession of them at that time. Moreover, he is likely to forget where he buried them. He is following instinctive behavior although he appears to be looking ahead. It is not here contended that none of the power to direct one's own evolvement is held by any creature other than man, but rather that he is the only one to possess such power in sufficient quantity to be effective. (15)

From man's capacity to remember and to foresee, he has come into possession of the wisdom as well as the folly of his forebears.

Since he knows to a degree what has happened and how it has worked out, he has learned to evaluate—that is, to judge of the effectiveness of past media and actions. The judgment of the past serves him in structuring the future. This process of evaluation has enabled him to develop a system of values, so that he has something against which to evaluate. (16)

The less man has been able, on his way up, to alter his circumstances the more fatalistic he has been. When he was completely at the mercy of the weather, he had little to say about his success or failure, so he accepted the point of view that what was to happen was foreordained. This fact explains why primitive man is fatalistic, and why those who struggle with the elements most closely are apt to hold similar beliefs. Before the invention of outside energy, man was so helpless in his effort to order his circumstances that he accepted the idea that what is to be is to be.

The ability to foresee, essential as it is to human progress, is not an unmixed blessing. It enables us to solve some problems, but it raises others. It carries with it responsibility, and resultant anxiety. One may know so much about what is going to happen that one cannot support the knowing. For example, one may worry oneself into a state of mental ill-health by contemplation of the possibilities of the atomic bomb. We cannot, however, cope with life by running away from it. (17)

Enough has already happened to convince us that man is increasingly able to order his circumstances, and to control the nature of his development. Since the creation of outside energy is so new and since its present possibilities are so great, the vision of a man-ordered world looms as a real prospect. The ability to remember and to foresee is the key to the next development in man. It is the reason for education, for if man cannot direct his own evolvement, he may as well take things as he finds them. (18)

4. THE FUNDAMENTAL METHOD OF PROGRESS IS COOPERATION

Perhaps there is no more widely held misconception in our modern industrial society than that the basic method of progress in all living things, including man, is competition. This is the idea that each must look out for himself, pretty much without regard for others. It is held that, if each looks out for himself successfully, all will be taken care of except the weaklings, who really do not matter much anyway. We can extend them our sympathy, but we can judge only that they are unfit for survival. The goods of earth belong to those who can take them. (19)

This attitude may in part be due to the fact that each of us has his own egoistic drives—his need to be a factor, to "have a place in the sun." The simplest approach to the satisfaction of this need would be simply to take his place, all he can get, without regard to the cost to others. This method of progress has been glorified as "rugged individualism." The transition from "rugged" to "ruthless" is short, and soon spanned. Indeed in our present society, ruthlessness is only slightly immoral, if at all. (20)

Charles Darwin, perhaps inadvertently, gave great impetus to this approach to progress with his ideas on the survival of the fittest. He painted a word picture of the plant and animal world struggling for space and food, with only the strongest succeeding and with death far more common than life. His ideas caught on and had tremendous influence because they seemed to justify the narrow egoistic approach to life, which, in this narrow concept, some people wanted to have justified. If man wanted to exploit his fellow, it was a comfort to have a great scientist discover from research that that is the way of all life. And so Darwin's survival of the fittest became almost a household saying, which in itself is a phenomenon, since scientific biological research is not often so successful.

Even those of us who saw value in cooperation as a way of life were inclined to concede that competition was the natural method of progress. We said that, even though this was true, the civilizing process involved the sublimation of this base natural demand and that man was civilized to the degree that he was able to rise above his natural egoistic drives and learn that his greatest good lay in the good of all. We thought of competition as the law of the jungle, not fully appreciating what actually goes on in the jungle.

We now know from biological research that the fundamental method of progress for living things is not competition, but cooperation. Life apparently started in the form of single-celled organisms. But the single-celled organisms we now know, such as amoeba or pleurococcus, are not importantly advanced over what the first cells must have been. When progress has been made, it has been made by cells associating themselves together, and then taking on specialized functions, so that not every cell any longer has to do everything for itself. As soon as the trick of sticking together for mutual advancement and that of specializing functions were hit upon, the possibilities of progress became infinite. It is fortunate for the predatory rugged individual that his separate cells do not decide to behave as he does. (21)

Early in the development of most human organisms they have abandoned asexual and developed heterosexual reproduction. Thus was made possible greater diversity of hereditary characteristics, and the introduction of the possibility of improved chromosome combinations. At the same time, heterosexual reproduction called for the cooperation of two separate multicellular individuals. No one can doubt that heterosexual reproduction has had much to do with the development of higher organisms; in fact, we can say that higher organisms as we know them could not have been developed purely by asexual reproduction. But if individuals refused to cooperate in this regard, and each went his own rugged way, organisms would have had to retain asexual reproduction or perish.

The very beginning, then, of an individual life depends upon the cooperation of separate individuals. In the human species, the newborn infant is so helpless that it cannot survive without further cooperation. The basis for relationships between individuals, the individuals' need for each other, and the resultant family and society have their beginning in this mother-infant relationship. (22)

The process of cooperation is obviously continued in other relationships between plants and animals. Examples of symbiosis, where different species live together in their mutual advantage, are endless. The lichen is a fungus and an alga living together, the fungus furnishing attachment and moisture for both, the alga manufacturing food for both. Experiments have shown that goldfish can survive adversity if there are several of them under conditions where a single one would perish. The wise gardener knows that he should not plant a single row of sweetcorn, but several shorter rows, in order to bring them together. Mutuality is now known to be almost a requirement among living things.

It is of course true that when too many organisms try to live in one spot, some will perish from sheer want of space and food. Since lower organisms are unable to direct their own evolvement, and since most plants are not mobile, this is sure to happen. But to consider this as a desirable condition or as a method of progress is to take a superficial view of what goes on. This view mistakes an unfortunate fact of location for a method of progress.

Some men, to be sure, try to "go it alone." They are not so independent as they fancy themselves to be, because they could not exploit if there was nobody to exploit. But it can be seen that they do not really grow in the direction of competent human beings. Their growth takes special forms demanded by their loneliness and they become different and peculiar. They are as the gnarled oak on the top of the mountain, fighting alone against the elements, in contrast to the tall straight oak of the forest, where other oaks have helped to ameliorate the assaults of wind and rain.

Man, then, is a social creature or he is nothing. He is an individual within the framework of his society. There is no proof that he is a social creature by nature of his genes, although there is a good probability that this is true. At the instant of birth he becomes a social creature, and he can never fulfill his possibilities in any other way. Others thus become as essential as food or shelter. Since others are essential, no man can be unmindful of others. Being mindful of others, seeing that others survive to fulfill one's social need, is the essence of cooperation.

CHAPTER 4

Man's Ways of Knowing

Archeology has enabled us to understand how from the moment when primitive human creatures shaped the first tools, chapter after chapter has been added to the tale of man's accomplishments. He masters fire, he discovers a mechanical principle, he becomes an artist, he learns to farm, to weave, to shape pots, to sail boats, to make wheels, to cast bronze, to work iron, until imperceptibly we have reached the unfinished chapter of tomorrow.

—Jackette and Christopher Hawks

We see the living organism, then, as a unit of energy seeking to spend itself. It possesses the capacity to convert energy in the form of food into energy in the form of organism, so that it can become larger or substitute new structure for old. The highest of these living organisms is developed to the point where it can remember and foresee, and thus control to a degree the circumstances under which it lives. The fundamental method of progress is social, or cooperative.

A great many of these living organisms have the power or capacity to know what is in their surroundings. We do not know just how far down the scale toward the one-celled creature this ability goes. It seems certain that many of the lower animals possess this power. It may even be that the amoeba has it to a minor degree. It is doubtless true that this capacity reaches its highest refinement in man.

What we know about our surroundings comes about through the phenomenon of perception. If there were no perception, we would be completely unaware of our surrounding media, and would therefore be helpless to accommodate ourselves to them or to modify them. We would be as the rocks, or perhaps as the trees—

31

the victims of whatever came our way. Perception is the key link between us and our environment. It is the precise point where knowing, and action based on knowing, is pointed up.

The nervous system in man, as well as in many other animals, has developed various receptors which are able to receive stimuli from surroundings. These receptors make use of light waves, sound waves, particles floating in air and liquids, and pressures. These are the simplest and most obvious forms of stimuli, and the ones we naturally know most about. There is some evidence that man receives other stimuli, often referred to as extrasensory, but we know little about them at this time. It is possible that some of the lower animals are more sensitive to these little-known stimuli than we are. We know, for example, that some animals can hear higher notes than we can. For us those stimuli do not exist.

When these stimuli have been received, most obviously through sight, hearing, touch, taste, and smell, the nervous system has developed ways of interpreting them and bringing them into consciousness, more or less in accordance with what actually lies in externality. Through this process, man is aware, or cognitive, of what lies about him. This is the first essential for effective action.

5. What We Know Comes From Us

The superficial interpretation of the phenomenon of perception has been that the organism is merely a receptor and that the perception came from the outside. If one saw a tree, the tree was the perception, since the tree started the chain of events. This interpretation implied that what was perceived was identical with what was outside. Since the tree was the perception, all organisms must see it alike.

We now know through laboratory evidence that the actual perception, that which comes into consciousness, comes from the organism itself, and not from the object in the externality. When we behold a tree, we see it in the light of all our tree experience. The plainsman sees one thing, the woodsman another. No two people see precisely the same thing, and in no individual case does the perception actually correspond with the tree. It is an interpretation made by the individual in the light of his experiences and purposes. (23)

What is real in any situation is not the object that started the sequence, for it can be many things to as many men, but the individual interpretation put upon it, for it is on this interpretation that the individual must act. The more closely his perception agrees with what actually lies outside him the more successful he will be. But the object itself will always remain what he makes it as he interprets the stimuli brought to him by his receptors.

The object that started the stimuli that resulted in the perception of course exists. Without it, there would have been no sequence. And most of the time, but not always, the perception is quite similar to the object. But this is not always true. Everyone has had the experience of seeing something totally different from what was seen at the same time by another person. Not knowing about the subjective nature of perception, this difference often leads to disputes.

Another striking example of this occurs when a person undergoes psychosis. In certain psychoses, it is possible for one to reject his surroundings completely, disregarding or misinterpreting all that comes to him through his receptors. He can thus build for himself completely new surroundings more in accord with his purposes. He can people those surroundings with those he wishes to see and to be with. This is only possible because of the fact that all our perceptions come from us, not from our externality, in accordance with our individual experience and purpose.

This fact becomes powerfully significant when we realize that through this process man is building his own experiences. Through his own misinterpretations he is becoming what he selects to become. Cognative life is thus seen to be almost entirely subjective. It is never objective except when we get out the measuring stick in order to find out whether the object we perceive is actually what we thought it was. Even after we have used the measuring stick we each reserve our own opinions concerning what we have been objective about. (24)

6. We Are Accumulated Experience

Man is able to direct his own evolvement, partly to make the circumstances that make him. This phenomenon is possible because he has developed the capacity to remember and to foresee.

These abilities come about through the high development of his central nervous system, the ultimate so far in cell specialization and cooperation.

Because he is able to remember, man is able to accumulate experience. He always perceives in the light of this accumulated experience, and he can perceive in no other way. This is a two-way process—he perceives what he is able to perceive in the light of his experiences up to the moment, and these perceptions are experiences. They are built into structure so that his next perception will be colored by them. Since experience is essential to perception, or to new experience, we must say that man is built by where he has been and what he has done. He is continually building himself by a combination of his past and his new surroundings or circumstances.

This gives meaning to the statement that, from a functional point of view, man is a bundle of experience, in flux or process, being continually modified or rebuilt as he makes his way in a changing world, or a world of new circumstances. His surroundings make him, and he at the same time makes his surroundings. Through his power to project into the future, or foresee, he has some power to say what conditions will make him. In dealing with his planned circumstances, he discovers that they will not function for him exactly as he had projected them, but that they will come more nearly doing so than if they had not been projected or planned.

The person who lives in a drab city may think he would like a flower garden to look out upon and to spend his time in. He plans and contrives, either by modifying his own back yard or by moving to a place where his dreams may be more possible of fulfillment. He may enjoy his garden immensely, but it is certain not to work out exactly as he had planned. He may find after he gets it that he really does not enjoy gardening as he thought he would. He has attempted to modify his circumstances in accord with a projected bit of foreseeing, and he has succeeded in part. What he becomes in his attitude toward the whole business of having a garden depends upon how the actual concrete project fitted his past experience.

Experience, then, is the process of undergoing, the contact with the concrete, the working out of projected circumstances. It is built into structure, and man is made out of it. The organism is henceforward different, and if it were possible to repeat an experience, the outcomes would be different, since the repeated experience would really be encountered the second time by a different individual. (25)

That is why it is not possible, even from a theoretical point of view, to have the same experience twice. The experiencer is not available for the test. Neither can two individuals, even identical twins, have the same experience, because what the person is makes the experience what it is.

To be sure, not all experiences are equally potent, and not all process modifies. We encounter innumerable coincidences every day which make no impression upon us at all because they lack significance to us as we are at that time. In order that an experience may modify the organism, it must have enough familiar elements so that there is some place to hitch on to old experiences which are built into the organism, and it must have enough novelty so that it can challenge attention. If there is nothing there which has not already been built into structure, no structure building will occur.

It might also be added that in our social world with its values, not all experience builds the structure in directions which will make the organism more adequate to live the social life as it must be lived if the individual is to make his way among other social beings. From the point of view of adequacy, an experience may be capable of building new structure, but the total reconstructed organism may be less adequate to make its way in a social, cooperative world. Such experiences are undesirable although perhaps potent, and they should be avoided as the individual looks forward and projects the circumstances that make him. It also follows that those who are helping plan for others toward competency and adequacy, as the adult plans for the young, need to take this into account.

In the light of what is now known about the interrelationship between the organism and environing circumstances, we are able to bring new understanding to some of our past research. The Iowa studies of the early 1930's, for example, showed that what we had called the IQ, which we had believed to be constant, was not constant at all, but varied with conditions. These studies showed that starved environments caused dull people, and that rich environments produced relatively bright people. Dullness and brightness are achievements, and not necessarily gifts. Such a conclusion is precisely what we would expect in the light of what we know about the interrelation of perception and experience. Those who are forced to live in undesirable conditions are caught in a downward spiral of cause and effect, and the organism thus built reflects the stuff out of which it is built.

There are those who will ask what place thinking—they usually like to call it reflective thinking—has in experience. Is it an experience?

It would seem that every conscious organism is undergoing experience of more or less significance, although it is possible that the "less" may be insignificant practically. As he goes forward, man reacts, evaluates, projects. Ordinarily it is an ongoing performance, as new experiences impinge. Sometimes he may go away by himself and consider the events of the past, but he has nothing to think with except his past experiences. He may seem to be withdrawn but he is prolonging what goes on all the time out in the current of events. Thinking is the organization, integration, and projection of experience, as well as being experience itself.

All experience thus has value as its inescapable accompaniment. What does the organism make of it? How did it work out? Is it thus to be sought or avoided? These evaluations are a running concomitant of experience, and thinking is part of the constant flow. What is built into structure is colored by value, or by what we think of it.

We perceive what we have experience and purpose to perceive, and that perception is built into us. Our future perceptions depend upon it. Thus experience is accumulated, and functioning structure is built.

7. Man Acquires Knowledge Through Experience

Perception, experience, thought, and value are so automatic and instantaneous that we have to look upon them as one process. Perhaps we ought to add emotion or attitude to this whole phenomenon, since we are probably never free from an emotion of some sort connected with an experience. Certainly it seems that we cannot evaluate without having a feeling of the goodness or badness of an experience in its effect upon us. This process is all part of the flow of life, and goes on whether we will it or not.

Because we have the ability to remember, an achievement of a highly developed nervous system, there is a residue of experience. Something is left after the experience is over. We have spoken of this residue as being built into structure, because the organism seems to be different thereafter. At least the organism does not behave the same as though it had not been through the experience, and so from a functional point of view it is different. Since we hold that a thing is what it does, structure has been modified.

What is left can be spoken of as knowledge. There is more to it than this, since there are attitudes, habits, conscious and subconscious feelings. The organism knows something it did not know before, if its memory is working, as a result of each significant experience. This something is what we mean when we speak of knowledge. It is simply what the organism knows.

This we believe to be the naïve concept of the word. In the hands of the philosophers and educators knowledge has come to take on a somewhat different meaning. They regard it as something set apart, mostly in books. It is similar to, and probably related to, the notion of perception in which the organism is held to be a receptor only, with the reality lying outside the organism. This view makes knowledge something which exists in its own right, and portrays the organism as acquiring it much as an amoeba flows around food. This concept holds knowledge to be the same no matter who acquires it.

From what is known about perception we can now see that knowledge does not exist before learning begins, but it is a product or residue of the learning process. Since the process itself is unique, knowledge resulting from it must also be unique. No two people therefore can know the same things, nor can any item of knowledge have the same effect on each of them. The experience through which the knowledge was acquired was personal, and so was the perception that made the experience possible.

Some will be disturbed by this concept, because it is contradictory to a deeply held notion which is basic to most of our present education. Is it not a fact, they may ask, that Abraham Lincoln lived, and that all good Americans should know about him? It is doubtless true that Lincoln lived, and from what we can learn most of us would benefit by experiences which would leave us a residue of knowledge about him. There are, however, as many Lincolns as there are learners. He is one thing to an Old Guard Republican, who holds him as a model but believes little that he believed. He is something else to the descendants of the slaves whom he freed. He is still another person to the southern aristocrat. We may argue, if we wish, that the fact of Lincoln exists apart from the learner, but this fact does not matter until Lincoln is taken in by a unique organism and is interpreted in the light of the experience and purpose of the learner. To some he does not exist at all, to others he is far from what we hold him to be. We may well wonder at this point what manner of man he was, and whose Lincoln is most like the man who lived in the nineteenth century. It seems certain that he will change through the generations, and it would be folly to predict what he will stand for in the minds of men by the year 3000.

Knowledge, then, is what we know. It is a product or residue of the perception-experience process. It is subjective in nature, and unique to the learner. It does not exist before learning begins, or if it does, that fact does not matter. It is a result of process, and is subject to continuous modification as process goes forward in a changing world. It is made possible through memory, and is uniquely held and uniquely used.

8. WE HAVE NO GIVEN COMMON WORLD

We now see the completely subjective nature of life. Because of the evolvement of heterosexual reproduction, the individual starts life with his own hereditary equipment. With this foundation, he begins to have his own perceptions, which come from him because of what he is. Through his own perceptions he accumulates experience unique to him and unlike that of any other person, and the residue of the experience is built into his structure.

Because of the manner by which these phenomena come about, what man perceives, what he knows, what he becomes is strictly his own and no other's. It is impossible for him ever to perceive anything exactly as others do. And so he lives in a world of his own, unshared in complete detail by his contemporaries. Therefore we come to the inescapable fact that we have no given common world with our fellow men. Each sees his own world, and makes his own interpretations, and the differences in this seeing build us differently.

This shows why it is so difficult for us to understand each other. It is difficult even between those who have much similarity of experience and much intimacy of association. The more varied the set of experiences from which we make our interpretations the more difficult it is to achieve understanding. That is why it is so difficult for us to understand the Russian people, for example, and so hard for them to understand us. But we do not need to go to the other side of the world for an illustration. The experiential background of the employer is usually so different from that of the laborer that they approach their mutual problems with quite different structures. Since each assumes a common world, each takes a blameful attitude toward the other, and can see nothing but perverseness on the part of the other because they do not see their problems alike.

This fact of knowing, or perhaps of not knowing, becomes extremely important when we consider that earlier we made the point that the primary task of the human organism is to make its way with other human organisms. We are nothing if not social—we are nothing by ourselves. We seem to search and to yearn for communion with others, never quite achieving it. This reaching out toward others is the natural effort of the organism to overcome its seclusion.

Some people, when they encounter the idea that we have no given common world, consider that fact extremely discouraging and productive of pessimism. They say that if this is true, then we have no basis on which to operate, no place to begin, and that the human race is therefore doomed to misunderstanding, strife, and war.

This is an overstatement of our dilemma. As we view history we see a great deal of strife and war, but we also see instances of success in human association. While we have no common world in that no one can have another's experience and therefore cannot have his attitude, we do have things in common, and it is they which form a point where we can begin to approach communion. We all have the earth ball on which we live, for example. Not that we view it the same, but the fact that we all start out, dwell, and die on the same earth gives us a starting point. We have innumerable things in common, and our perception can be brought nearer and nearer to correspondence with externality. When we all work to improve our perception of the same object, we come nearer and nearer to commonalty.

Also we have means of communication between separate and different organisms. The greatest of these is language. It is true that any one language admits us only to a portion of the other human beings on earth, and that with many we have almost no way of communicating. Even with those using the same language, we have difficulty conveying meaning because each has his own subjective interpretation of words. Language can, however, become a greatly improved tool of communication when we recognize that lack of communication is our real problem, and put our minds to the improvement of language.

While we have no *given* common world, we have a way of gaining a large degree of commonty. This way is the working toward more complete understanding with others through improved communication. Communication is best achieved when people work together toward common goals. The goals serve as guide-posts for action, not as ends. When sought goals are achieved, new ones are seen. Commonty is not *given*, but must be worked at, and practical understanding can thus be gained. (26)

The principal note of optimism lies in the fact that we now come to see the basic difficulties in human relations. This is encouraging because we never can start to fix anything until we see what is the matter with it. Even if it should take a thousand years to fix it, we can feel better when we know what our trouble has been and are on the way toward a remedy. As long as we do not know why human beings behave as they do, and why they have drifted into conflict, we are at a loss to know where to begin.

Man's way of knowing, then, is through the phenomenon of perception, by which he becomes cognizant of his surroundings. This is subjective and not objective. Through his ability to remember, he is able to accumulate experience, and at least the conscious part of this storage is knowledge. Since perception and experience are subjective and personal, the residual knowledge also is subjective and personal. This fact gives him a world all his own, and makes his problem one of establishing communication with others living in unique worlds, to the end that sufficient understanding will result that life will be tenable.

CHAPTER 5

Man and His Environment

It is not only because of their endless variety that men are baffling. Each individual is baffling. How explain the gorgeous versatility of Shakespeare or Bach? Who can elucidate Abraham Lincoln? What key will unlock the inner secrets of Victoria Woodhull or Mary Baker Eddy? Is there a net to catch the volatile spirit of Lawrence of Arabia? Every biography is a post mortem performed upon a body that is dead.

—Max Otto

We have seen, in our discussion of perception, that man is equipped to take his environment into account. This enables him to cope with his environment, making use of those factors which can be turned to his advantage, and forfending where adverse conditions are encountered. While he is doing this, the process of experiencing is going on, and, due to the peculiar nature of perception, these experiences are continuously building him into what he is to become. Man's surroundings, then, become important in that they are the stuff out of which he is built. We need now to concern ourselves with the problem of man and his surroundings, to see how he relates himself to them, and what the final relationship between him and his environment is to be.

9. EACH INDIVIDUAL IS UNIQUE

The concept of the individual's uniqueness is not a startling one. Probably there is no one who would deny it. We can all of us see it all about us. As the teacher looks at her classroom full of children, there is nothing so obvious as the fact that no two of them are alike. They are tall and short, fat and thin, light and dark, alert and lethargic. We know and accept the idea that this uniqueness is found throughout nature.

Even in the inorganic world, this uniqueness seems to exist. Crystals form, but there are no two exactly alike. A sand dune contains billions of grains of sand, but under magnification it becomes obvious that to find two grains exactly alike would be hopeless. Nor would it be any easier to find two blades of grass in a field or two leaves in a forest that were exactly alike.

Up to now, however, the concept of uniqueness seems to have been a static one. For the most part, we have not made use of it. It has not been brought into concreteness through action. This can again be illustrated by the teacher, who knows her children are all different but who acts as though they were alike. Perhaps she acts this way because they all wear the same label, such as 4th grade. We have acted upon likenesses, which do indeed exist, although it seems likely that the significant feature is difference rather than similarity.

We now have better knowledge of the causes for uniqueness and of its significance. We can now see how deep it goes, whereas we had previously taken it as a superficial fact based on casual observation. Perhaps a better understanding of its importance will help to bring the concept into concreteness, where we can act upon it, rather than behaving as though it was not true.

The first guarantee of uniqueness comes from the fact of the bisexual nature of human origin. As long as reproduction was by fission, each new generation was a piece of the old, and there was no chance for much modification. It is true that there were modifying factors, such as climate and food supply, but there was little provision for change in the basic make-up of the cell.

With the development of bisexual reproduction, it is practically impossible for any two individuals except identical twins to have the same cellular construction. In human beings the cell contains 48 chromosomes. In ordinary cell fission, these chromosomes are split lengthwise, so that each new cell gets half of each chromosome. When the reproductive cell (the egg or sperm) is formed, the chromosomes line up in pairs, so that each new egg or sperm gets 24 of them. Which 24 the particular gamete will get is a matter of chance. When two gametes fuse in conception, that is, when the sperm penetrates and fuses with the egg to form the first cell of the new individual, the cell then again has 48 chromosomes.

Half of them are from the male and half from the female. The new organism is literally a combination of the two parents. (27)

The provision for uniqueness here is infinite. The two parents were unique to themselves in the whole world to begin with. The particular chromosome content of each gamete was a matter of chance with very low probability of a similar alignment giving similar gametes. Which sperm will find which egg is a matter of chance. We do not need to go into the mathematics of the matter in order to show that it is practically beyond the realm of the possible that there could ever be two individuals with the same foundation in chromosomes.

So no two individuals start out alike at conception, even less so at birth, but differentiation has only begun. Unlike most of the lower animals, the human infant is unfinished at birth. The helplessness of the newborn human being is well known, but the significance of this state of helplessness and incompleteness has not always been understood.

The young chicken, for example, is ready to launch itself as a chicken the moment it emerges from the shell. It is complete, ready to walk, to scratch, to peck. Except for size and feathers, which could hardly be packed in an egg that a hen could lay, it is what it is going to be. Its nervous system is all established. The nerves are sheathed, and thus not subject to impingement of circumstances. For weal or woe, it is set to go, and if what it is does not suit the conditions under which it is hatched, it will perish.

The human infant could not be said to be an adult in miniature. It hardly resembles the adult at all. Unlike the chick, it cannot do anything for itself except to take food which is thrust into its mouth. It can scarcely even reach for it. All these shortcomings are apparent. What is not apparent is that its nerves are unsheathed, and the growth of sheaths will not be completed for some time. Lack of nerve sheaths means much greater sensitivity to the impingement of circumstances and much more possibility for growth and improvement. There is an equal possibility for adverse development under adverse conditions. The potential for change is high, whereas in the chick there is almost no potential at all except the physical one. That is, the better nurtured the chick is the faster it will become a large healthy adult, but no other possibility exists.

As the infant begins to develop, the powers of memory and foresight begin to come into play. As these develop, the young individual begins to have and to exercise choice in the expenditure of its energy. This choice has a great potential in determining the particular direction growth will take. The wide possibilities for direction inevitably increase uniqueness. The chick must act as though it contained a set of springs. It has no choice but to scratch and to peck. It has no potential for varied paths of development.

Uniqueness is further guaranteed by the wide variety of circumstances under which the infant starts life. The spot on earth where birth happens to take place makes a great deal of difference. The era in which one is born, the climate, the type of available food, are all contributing factors. The kind of government under which one is born may limit the individual's imagination as to what good government may be like. Perhaps most important of all, the kind of people one happens to fall in with has much to do with the kind of individual that can develop. Since life consists of other people, and since the business of life is that of making one's way with them, the family and friends of the family become the most important factor in determining the direction of growth. (28)

The greatest modifier of all, perhaps, is experience. The individual soon starts having experiences as we know them, although prenatal life has provided experiences of a sort. These experiences come about through action and through the development of the powers of perception. Each significant experience is built into structure so that one becomes what one's experience has been, modified and interpreted by one's foundational structure.

No two persons can have the same experience, since the experience is what it is because of the peculiar unique structure and background that the individual brings to it. It is not the event alone which constitutes an experience but the interaction beween the event and the experiencing organism. To illustrate, two children might be spanked for some prank, and we might say that they had the same experience. Assuming that it was possible to deal out the same number of licks with the same intensity (which it is not), the two children would not have the same experience because one of them is certain to be more sensitive than the other, one is likely to have had more experience with this type of ordeal than the other, one has related himself to the spanker differently than the other, and so on for an infinite number of possibilities.

We can say, then, that no two individuals can, or in the normal course of events will, have the same experiences. Experience builds structure and we become what we must become in the light of what we have experienced. The flow of life begins at once on unique individuals to build them more uniquely. (29)

Nature, to employ a familiar abstraction, must love differences and abhor sameness, since she has gone to such lengths to provide differences and to see to it that samenesses literally cannot exist. The statistically perfect oak leaf probably does not exist. The straight line is an abstraction and does not exist in nature. The complicated phenomenon of bisexual reproduction must have been extremely difficult to come by, and living organisms must have sorely needed the differentiation and specialization made possible by it.

We see, then, new and clearer reasons for the old cliché that says people are different. We have long known that each individual had his own chromosome content, unlike even his own siblings', and we used to say that for that reason people grew up to look different from each other. What we have come more recently to understand is the uniqueness of perception, which controls experience, and that experience is actually and verily built into structure. We see now more clearly the scientific basis for uniqueness. The result should be a more potent understanding of it. This understanding may result in the concept coming out of the abstract, and becoming a concretion by which we live.

10. Each Individual Is Uniquely Related to His Externality

We started Part I with the concept of change as the fundamental law of the universe. We have presented the individual as a knowing, perceiving, experiencing organism, able to take his environment into account, and to foresee consequences. This gives us a concept of the unique human organism in a situation of flux, continuously taking into account the everchanging situation, something like a fish swimming upstream. There is no other fish in the world exactly like this one, and the flowing water that he strives with carries ever different other fish and debris for his attention or for his ignoring. The banks and the bottom of the stream, the swiftness of the current, the temperature of the water, are continuously different and continuously carry the potential of "for better or for worse."

As the individual goes forward in this inevitable and inescapable stream of life, he relates himself uniquely to the ever-changing stream of things and people. He cannot do other than relate himself uniquely, because he is unique and the circumstances in which he finds himself are unique. How he relates himself to things and people can now be seen to be one of the most important things about any individual.

We have seen that the organism is a unit of energy seeking to spend itself in accordance with its own structure, experientially arrived at, and with its own purposes. How the organism relates itself to the things and people of its externality reveals the lines of energy expenditure which is life itself. In large measure, we choose what we will relate ourselves to, and what the nature of that relationship will be. Thus we reveal the lines along which our energy, literally pieces of ourselves, will be spent. This revelation of the lines of energy expenditure is perhaps the most enlightening factor in coming to know about the inner workings of an individual. It is the stock in trade of the effective teacher, physician, social worker, psychiatrist, as well as that of all other people who strive to make their way with other human beings. (30)

There are many factors which we hold in common, particularly in the world of things, and to which we make similar (but not the same) relationships. We have mentioned the earth ball on which we live as being something held in common. We are all subject to the law of gravitation, and all are obliged to function under it. This law is a great boon to life, since we do not have to concern ourselves with the problem of remaining on the earth. It gives us position from which we can view and take into account the stream of people and things. We would indeed be in flux if we could not count on that. Since we are in a moving stream, we have little enough to count on without worrying about that problem. It may be that the stability given us by gravity is the factor that makes so many of us erroneously believe that we can find a firm foundation on which to stand.

There are many other conditions which are in a similar category. Most of us, though not all, are subject to the succession of day and night. We thus have habituated ourselves to periods of activity and of rest. It might have been mentioned in Chapter 1 that another upsetting of age-old habits has come about through the development of artificial light almost equal to daylight, and the resultant turning of night into day. This change is another product of our newly discovered energy supply outside our own bodies. We also have the contours of the earth's surface in common, to which we make similar adjustments. Through the ages man has adjusted to earth crust as he found it, mountains, valleys, rivers, oceans, or plains. More recently in human history we have altered contours with such things as tunnels and dams, which we hold more or less in common.

The great variable in the stream of life is the other people whom the individual must encounter. The chief business of life, as we have said, is to make one's way with other human beings. Life is social, or it is almost nothing. In this fact lies the great potential for variation, and we can now see how extremely complicated the variation is. Each human being is unique, and each is uniquely related to all others. This matter of being uniquely related would be true even if we were all alike, because physical position would account for it. Two persons cannot occupy the same space at the same time, and therefore no two persons can be similarly related, even in space and time, to other individuals. When considering a desirable or undesirable other object or person there is a great difference between near and far. When we add to this all the potential of unique heredity, experience, and purpose held by both organisms so related, the real situation of relatedness becomes very complicated.

These variables determine whether two persons hold each other to be friend or foe, asset or liability. When a new person floats within one's perceptive reach, each brings all his yesterdays to bear upon what his attitude will be. Whether they hold each other

in trust and confidence or in suspicion and fear makes the difference in what can come out of the propinquity. Too often this attitude or this relatedness is quickly and almost automatically
established out of experience and previous attitude on similar
occasions. This relatedness can be revised through experience, but
such revision takes time and effort.

That it must be worked at is evident from what we know about
cooperation as the method of progress for all living things. We cannot go it alone, and therefore the way in which we pick up relationships with other human beings as they come into our sphere of
comprehension will determine how successful we will be in the
primary business of living. The apparatus for picking up new
human relatedness must always be in working condition because
we cannot hold any one individual within our orbit throughout
life. If we cannot so hold an individual, and if we do not establish
new relatedness, we are eventually alone, and that is to say that
we have ceased to live in any significant way.

The need for successful relatedness can be illustrated in many
ways. Successful relatedness is essentially the business of getting
on good enough terms with other people so that cooperation, essential to all that live, can be achieved. The most elemental form
of this cooperation, because survival of the race depends upon it,
is that of mating. We all know both men and women who have
related themselves so badly in the highly charged area of sex that
they have been unable to achieve procreation. We must have some
form of government which implements the way we want to live.
Government calls for a degree of agreement made possible by a
relationship. In our complex society we have to agree upon and to
accept specialization. This means that an individual has his
specialized contribution to make to the general good, and has a
willingness to accept and to use the specialization of others.

There is a further requirement that we get together in the realm
of aspiration. To promote a better society we need to have common ideals, made possible through tenable relationships. We hold
visions of a better world, seen by people so related that they can
imagine together. We have need for community of interest in religions, held in common by numbers of people, and bearing upon
ways in which life may be better lived, and ways by which transfer

to another kind of life may be possible. Similar communion is required in the conception and development of aesthetics.

How one relates himself to things and to people, especially the latter, determines how successful one will be in the primary business of life. What we hold others to be in attitude, based upon all we have to bring to the relatedness, determines how well we will make out. What we see when another floats into our ken establishes the basis for what relation may occur. If a human being is to improve his success in making his way, it is precisely at this point that he must do it. The individual can do something about it himself through self-analysis. Those who work with others can best attack their problems at this point. That relatedness can be modified by self and others makes valid the hopes for a better world. (31)

We come to see that if we are to live, others must live also, and since very life depends upon others, humankind is all one, and what happens to another also happens to us. We can see how it is that the most important thing about any person is his attitude toward other people. (32)

11. Man and His Environment Are One

Because the simplest approach to life has seemed to be the analytical one, man has for a long time habituated himself to analysis. This process has indeed been helpful in the solution of many of his problems, but it has had a tendency to lead him away from a feeling for what now appears to be his basic nature. We are coming to see that man is a unitary being, and can really only succeed as he understands what it means to be a unitary organism. The now apparently valid concept of life as process calls for a unitary approach to the problems of life.

In the process of analysis, and under the control of this deep-seated habit, man has created a long series of dualities. Everything had to come by opposites. The concept of dualities is essentially contrary to the unitary concept, and it is proving itself false. As we go along in the understanding of the human organism in its environment, one by one the long-held dualities fall by the wayside. In time we may have none left.

We will not need to cite here all the dualities to which man has habituated himself. To do so would be exhausting and unrewarding. Two or three of them will suffice to show that they are not tenable. One of the commonest is that of body and mind. The mind has been held to reside in the brain, and to be something quite different in entity and function from the body. We are coming to realize that there is no such separation. The brain is a group of specialized cells with a special task to perform for the good of the whole. But when we have a feeling we feel it all over. If it is violent enough, we feel it in our digestive tracts. Sick bodies cause sick minds, and sick minds cause sick bodies. It is truer and easier to say that when the organism is sick, it is sick all over.

Psychiatrists know this, and it is their basic point of attack. Physical symptoms are explained in terms of memory, or attitude, or wish. Outside of psychiatry, physicians are coming to practice psychosomatic medicine, and to use the psychiatric approach in limited form. When the organism responds, it responds with brain, heart, stomach, and toe. The cure of many of our ills lies in the treatment of the real cause, which is to be found in the realm of attitude and emotion. It may come about that all our ills may eventually be solved in this way. There is a temptation to say at this point that the body does what the mind wants it to do, but the very statement would make use of the duality that we are in process of denying. We ourselves are so habituated to analysis and to duality that we fall unconsciously into their use.

We have held a duality which we have called subjective-objective. So-called scholars and scientists take great pride in their objectivity, and they usually consider subjectivity to be bad. We can see, though, from what we know about the individual nature of man's ways of knowing, and from the fact that we have no given common world, that nearly all of life is subjective, and the things that really matter are all subjective. We strive for a workable degree of objectivity, but it is in degree only, and is never completely so. It seems likely now that the only complete objectivity exists in the abstract. Such things as numbers and straight lines are abstractions drawn from situations in nature. These and similar abstract symbols seem to be nearly all of our objectivity. Thus disappears, at least for practical purposes, another duality.

Thought and action have long been held to be two separate processes. Man was considered to think what he was going to do, and then do it. Or, it has been claimed that the way to do the best thinking was to retire from the active scene and do thinking by itself. The nature of the thinking and acting processes now show us that thinking and acting are one. There is no significant thinking apart from action of some sort. The place to do the most significant thinking is in the turmoil of life itself. When so-called reflective thinking occurs, it has to do with recent action. Men and institutions that attempt to isolate themselves from the stream of life get into eddies or stagnant pools, and the ivory tower viewed by those in the stream comes to look a little strange. The disappearance of the duality of thought and action is upon us, and it will have a modifying effect upon much that we do, especially in education. (33)

The duality with which we are primarily concerned here is that of man and his environment. This is a separation most firmly held. This duality may relate to the mistaken notion of perception, for externality has been thought to have reality in its own right—that the reality lay in the objects outside the organism and the organism was considered to be only a receptor. The naïve and perhaps superficially logical view is to say that of course man is one thing, his environment is another, giving us one more duality born of analysis based on insufficient or inaccurate data.

We now see that no such division can exist. In order to have a duality there must be a dividing line. Even in the simplest matters of obvious material things we are unable to say that at any given point the organism leaves off and the outside begins. A morsel of food lies on a plate in front of a person. It would seem to belong to externality. When it is swallowed, it is much the same except that it is inside the organism. A process of absorption begins, and part of the food eventually becomes organism. At what point does it cease to be externality and become organism? The air about us is part of us, coming and going. Even the climate is part of us as it functions in the building of structure. People often actually look like the climate in which they have developed.

These are simple facts, easily understood. The physical examples of interchange are not the most crucial facts of oneness. When we consider that the universe is an embodiment of energy of which man is only one expression, we can see that, whatever appearances may be, we are of the same stuff as our surroundings, and that all the energy inside and outside us is bent upon expenditure in those ways which are possible in the light of its particular form.

Most powerful of all, perhaps, is the idea that we are built out of experience. We are the product of what has happened to us, or what we have made happen. Since our perceptions come from us, that which is outside us is what we make it, and we perceive what we have experience and purpose to perceive. The very externality that we have so long tried to define and to describe by itself is not only part of us, but it is made by us. This quite completes the picture of oneness. It is the logical conclusion to be drawn from the fact that reality lies in perception, and the world we see is the world we can see considering what we have to see with. Two individuals standing together view two different worlds, and so there are two different environments, each one with the particular observer. If the duality existed, each would have to see the same world.

Continuously becoming oneness seems to be the process of integration. Integration is a formative process through which energy is able to work toward a goal. This formative process serves to unite man with nature, of which he is a part. Integration means unification, and since we know that the whole universe is on the move, that unity can come about only through formative process. (34)

We recently observed a group of city high school students in a camping situation on a forest conservation project. They had lived all their lives in the abstract setting of sidewalks, streets, apartments, bottled milk, and paper money. When they got out on the soil, their whole personalities seemed to develop while we watched. They showed a yearning to get close to the earth, and to unite with the soil from which they had sprung. Many of the frustrating and contending attributes that had developed while they were away from their mother earth seemed to disappear, and growth in the direction of integration literally broke forth. The longing for unity subconsciously held was here vigorously manifested.

Unity moves toward formative integration; divisiveness moves toward disintegration. The process of integration-disintegration is a further explanation of change, which is the dynamic for the whole universe. There was energy before there was anything else. Energy has taken the form of substance. Substance has become animate, some of the animate has become man. Man and environment are one because they are made of the same stuff and one is constantly in process of becoming the other. (35)

So we can no longer speak of man and his environment as two separate entities. Since this is true, function becomes more important than form—what man does, rather than what he appears to be, becomes crucial. This concept of unity has great bearing on man's concept of himself, and the way by which he can best build a unified world for himself.

CHAPTER 6

All Living Tissue Is Purposive

Every plant and animal thus acts as an incorporating center which brings organic order out of environmental chaos.

—Edmund Sinnott

Our conclusions that life processes are essentially and fundamentally directive and creative may be rejected as "metaphysical" or "mystic." It is of course nothing of the sort. I make no hypothesis as to the physical philosophical basis or "ground" of directiveness and creativeness. I merely accept the patent evidence that they are characteristic of living things and of them alone.

—Bertrand Russell

The word "purpose" has already crept into the text. We have needed the word and the concept in order to make the account hang together. We have not wanted to use it before we could explain it. This is a dilemma in writing. Books are linear, one page must follow another, but the material is not linear. It is more like a ball, with many string ends on it, any one of which may serve for the unraveling. Perhaps one cannot hope to establish a completely logical order of ideas when all are interdependent, and when there is need to tell them all at once. Fortunate is the fiction writer, who can tell a story as it happened in time. This story, if it may be called one, cannot be told in that way. Perhaps a good deal of the misunderstanding among men comes from the fact that they are always required, by the nature of communication, to make spherical things linear.

We need the concept of purpose in order to explain the phenomena of living things. This concept is not something we can isolate in a test tube or view under a microscope. It is no less real on that account. Science has always invented concepts and even structures to conform with the behavior of matter. This is a thoroughly respectable device. No one, for example, has even seen an electron, but electrons are as real to the physicist as though they had been seen. They have to exist, else matter would not behave as it does. Living things have to purpose in order for us to account for their behavior.

An illustration may prove helpful. We have said that the phenomenon of perception, which is the organism's link to his externality, and therefore the most fundamental factor in human life, is based on experience and purpose. That is, we see what we have experience to see, and what we purpose to see. It is not enough to say merely that we see what we have experience to see, because experience alone is not enough to account for what happens.

Let us suppose that two persons are standing together viewing a casual scene. It might be a pastoral scene, with field, wood, stream, animals. Both have had experience with virtually everything in the scene. They are confronted with thousands of coincidences in the scene. Each will see something different, and will choose a very few of the many coincidences to observe. Why do they not select the same ones? Or why do they not select all for which they have the experiential background? The only answer that seems adequate is that from an experiential point of view they might have, but they had different purposes. Purpose, then, becomes an essential in the transaction of perception itself, the key to social living. Many other phenomena require the existence of purpose to make them comprehensible. (36)

The term "purpose" needs defining, or at least requires an explanation as to how it is used here. The term is loosely used in general conversation to mean several different things. It may mean a conscious goal of the moment. "I want to play golf this afternoon" might be an example. It may be confused with the goal itself. Or it may be used as a verb, such as "I purpose to buy a suit." These are all superficial and inaccurate (or varying) uses of the term.

What we mean by the term "purpose" is a driving force which gives expression for, or points a path to, the expenditure of the energy of which we consist. In lower forms it is always below consciousness, and in man, the most conscious of all organisms, it is mostly, but not always, below consciousness. It has been customary to refer to unconscious purpose as drive, but since it appears to be one thing only, it seems better to use one word for it. (37)

Purpose protrudes into consciousness when we are not sure of, or completely satisfied with, a prospect, and we feel that it needs to be validated. Unconscious purposes are set up to operate automatically and have been put on a closed circuit, perhaps because they work so well. Conscious purpose may be modified within limits. The limits are that no activity which violates the deeper unconscious purposes of the organism can become a true conscious purpose. (38)

For example, my neighbor may want me to go fishing with him. I do not want to go, perhaps because I have never been fishing and can have no feeling for its pleasures. But he is persistent, and finally I consent to go. At this point, fishing is not my purpose. I am doing something through coercion for another reason. I may figure that if I go once, he will be satisfied and will stop bothering me about it. It may come about that I enjoy it very much, and want to go again. I may soon be found coercing others to go with me. (39)

In like manner, in the hands of a skillful parent or teacher, a child may come to accept as his purpose some enterprise or some learning which in the beginning was not included in his purpose. The worth of the enterprise for him will be determined by the degree to which it can become a fully accepted purpose in keeping with the deeper functioning of his unique organism.

By far the more fundamental and powerful force is unconscious purpose. When we speak of conscious and unconscious purpose, we do not mean that they constitute another duality; we believe them to be all one phenomenon. Conscious purpose is that manifestation of purpose which thrusts itself into the conscious. It is less well established, more tentative, more in need of validation, and more subject to modification than that part of purpose which never needs to come to consciousness. The unconscious purpose may be called tissue purpose, since there is evidence of it existence in all living tissue, and since it operates in a human being much the same as in a tomato plant. It may be that the philosophers who labored over the will, who made will a noun, and set it up as a faculty of the mind, were really concerned with tissue purpose, with the directional guide to the expenditure of the energy that constitutes the tissue. If there is similarity, we see now that it is not a faculty residing in the brain, but it is the very force out of which living tissue and all other matter are made. (40)

So far as we can now see into the mystery of motivation and of behavior, there seems to be a difference between living and non-living matter in this regard. When we are able to peer further into the nature of the processes involved, we may be able to see that they are not different, but the same. Now it looks as though energy spending in nonliving matter is toward disintegration, while in living matter it is toward integration. The insensate rock seems to be going from an order of sorts to disorder, or a returning to simpler organization, while all living things seem to be spending themselves in the direction of higher order, of more complexity, of greater specialization.

There seems to be a good deal of evidence that purpose is provided for in the genes. These are complicated molecules, with atom arrangements which have much to do with the nature of the organism, and doubtless control to a marked degree the way in which energy will be spent, as well as the vigor of the expenditure. These genes are the "building block and building plan." As the sperm and egg are infinitely unique, so, then, is the purpose. There is such overwhelming provision for uniqueness that the wonder is that individuals of one species are so much alike. Something holds the whole together, else the newly formed zygote might grow into any one of an infinite number of possible organisms. Knowing nature's profligate capacity for variation, it could be possible that no two zygotes would grow in the same direction of all. This, of course, does not happen. Human beings beget human beings, frogs beget frogs. Life depends upon similarities as well as upon differences. (41)

Purpose is apparent in all plants and animals. The sperm seeks the egg, and rather determinedly too. This is true in human beings, but it is even more strikingly true in some plants. What a busy place a cornfield must be after the tassels and silks have come out! The sperm cell produced in the tassel has to land on the tip of a strand of corn silk, and must bore its way the whole length of the silk to get to the egg cell reposing on the cob. For every good ear of corn, row upon row of sperm cells have succeeded in reaching their goals. This performance shows a miracle of determination scarcely equaled in the realm of conscious purpose, even among the go-getters.

Evidence of tissue purpose in plants is everywhere about us. It appears to be a universal, best explained by the nature of energy and together with some sort of control laid down when the chromosome content of the new individual was determined. We all know, for example, that a plant set in a window will turn toward the light. This urge is so strong that it will distort the plant if left to operate too long, so we usually turn the plant occasionally in order to bring it back to some degree of symmetry. The roots have an equally strong urge, but that is in the direction of water. Some tree roots will grow through many feet of soil in order to reach a moist spot. Botanists have passed this fact off by saying the stem is phototropic, the root hydrotropic. This explanation merely gives a name to a phenomenon without explaining anything. These names serve no purpose except perhaps brevity, and occasionally they become so long that they do not even accomplish that. (42)

What we need to know in order to understand life is why the leaves turn toward the light, why the sperm seeks the ovum. If we can come to know the basis, or the why, of tissue purpose, we will understand many of the secrets of life. We are not at that stage now, but we do observe a universal phenomenon.

In humankind, starting with the fused sperm and ovum, we see tissue purpose operating all the way through prenatal and postnatal life. Perhaps the prenatal phenomena are most interesting because we have so long regarded the newborn babe to be a tabula rasa, at least from the standpoint of experience. Those who seek to reject the idea of the experiential nature of human development usually ask, quite triumphantly, "How, then, does the newborn babe get his first experience?" A discussion of this point is somewhat like that of the number of angels that can dance on the point of a needle, but the answer to the query comes clear when we consider the purposeful sperm cell and all that has happened in the previous nine months. (43)

During this time, all kinds of plans have been made for the life that is to be led in an altogether different medium. The fetus lives in liquid, the postnatal organism in air. The prenatal creature forms lungs before there is air to breathe. It forms eyes before there is light for them to receive. And so at birth the human organism has a sizable backlog of experiences, going way back to the eager sperm. That all or nearly all of this experience is unconscious does not affect its validity. So far as we know, all the experience of the corn plant, for example, throughout life is below the conscious level.

We like to think that, as adults, we are in charge of all decisions, and are the captains of our fate. And yet there is more operation of the human organism that is below the conscious level, and controlled by tissue purposes, than lies in the area of the conscious. Most of those functions which make us tick have been sealed off, immersed in brine similar to that in which we probably started life, and we have no control over them at all. The whole assembly of smooth muscles and the nerves that service them operate by themselves. We have no control over the heartbeat, digestion, sorting out of excretions, temperature controls, glandular secretions, and many other functions. We have some control over breathing, but not completely so. Only the activities of the striped muscles come into consciousness. We can therefore decide that we will play a game of golf, and can command our legs and arms to perform, but we have nothing to say as to whether the heart will carry us around the course. We are the captains of our fates in the degree that the purposes of our tissues permit.

We see, then, that we operate in accordance with a powerful unconscious force which is with us from the beginning and which controls in large part what we do. It is the factor that, added to a backlog of experience, determines the selections made in perception, and controls what is real to each individual. It serves as an unconscious judgment on the part of the organism as to what outside him is desirable and is to be sought, what is inimical and is to be fought or avoided, and what is irrelevant. Most of his surroundings are irrelevant and are ignored.

Situations for which we have no automatic answers come into consciousness. They are the tentative and the unvalidated. They may not always remain so, for when an action serves, and serves again, it may be relegated to habit. Acts performed through habit are not altogether unconscious, but lie in the realm between the conscious and the unconscious, since once they needed validation, but no longer do so.

Change is the basic law of the universe. It is inevitable because of the nature of living and nonliving matter, which is constituted of energy seeking to spend itself. In living matter, at least, the paths of expenditure are unique, and so change is unique. This expenditure of energy along prescribed paths is a force which we call purpose. In retrospect it becomes experience, and it is temporarily stabilized in that the organism is built by it.

It would seem, then, that all organisms can best and most fruitfully spend themselves in accordance with these unique lines of individual purpose, and that efforts to get the organism to spend itself contrarily will meet with frustration, both on the part of the spending organism and on the part of the organism seeking to divert the expenditure. Perhaps all that ever happens under this duress is that the individual changes his conscious goals, but not his unconscious purpose, over which he has no control, to meet a situation which he hopes will be temporary. In the case of a human being that is born and dies in slavery, it is not temporary; that is, it lasts as long as the individual does.

The driving force of tissue purpose (unconscious purpose) shows the path through which energy may be spent with complacence and satisfaction. It predates birth, and controls far more action than up to now we have supposed. It points the way by which the good life for any unique individual may be lived. It is the force through which the plant, the animal, the human being becomes more perfectly that which it already is. (44)

* * * * *

The facts set forth as headings in Part I seem to be true at the middle of the twentieth century. Whether they will stand up under further scientific scrutiny only time will tell. Surely some of them will be modified as we go forward, if we can judge by what has happened to most of the facts we have held to be true at any given time in the past. At any one point in the flow of time, we are compelled to take the facts we have at that time and base our actions upon them. So we must now consider how that which at present seems to be true affects practice. He who acts in as logical a manner as possible in the light of present knowledge is behaving intelligently and scientifically. He who bases his actions on ideas other than known facts is still behaving animistically.

The scientific method is the method whereby we look to nature to see how things behave, and postulate on that basis. We usually look upon Galileo and Kepler as the originators of this method, although we know there were many instances of its use before their time. They gave it the impetus that has created what we speak of as modern times. The dropping of the balls from the Tower of Pisa is a neat simple illustration of the scientific approach. It had always been assumed that a heavy object would fall faster than a light one. Galileo did not accept this fact as true without evidence. He looked to the balls for his belief. When he demonstrated the fact that the heavy and light balls fell at the same speed, even those who observed it would not believe it, but said that those particular balls were possessed of devils.

This point of view, held almost universally before the time of Galileo, is animistic, as opposed to scientific. It places spirits, or devils, in things which make them behave as they do. When a great event occurs, those who think animistically simply add power and wisdom to the spirit that made it possible. While we now think of our age as the age of science, we still have many people who are animistic, and perhaps all of us are at one time or another. There are probably few people in the world who are completely free from superstition. Superstition is the attributing of supernatural powers to things, beyond what we could expect from what we know about them. We still have many teachers who act on habit, or tradition, and who invest their wares with mythological powers in complete disregard of the known facts gained from scientific research.

Ever since the scientific method—the method of looking to things and to causes—has come into use, it has been opening doors for the human race. Even though the method did not come into general use for a long time, and is not universally used now, it has been used by people in laboratories, and it has enabled them to produce things which have modified life. The discoveries that have modified life most have been those which have added to the energy available to man for his use. The invention of the steam engine increased production of usable goods and facilitated movement. When we came to understand electricity, and saw how the electric spark could be used to ignite vaporized liquid fuel, the internal-combustion engine was born. This made possible the modern automobile, which has changed our conditions of living enormously. Now we are about to possess a far more vast supply of energy through atomic fission. It would be foolish indeed to attempt to predict what doors this may open to us, or how we shall presently be living as a result of it.

The recent facts we have about the nature of the human organism must surely open new doors for us in areas of learning and of human relations. Two or three illustrations may give point to this idea.

The new knowledge as to the nature of perception may affect us as much in the area of learning and human relations as the advent of the scientific method did in the area of tools, artifacts, and usable energy. This knowledge, once commonly held and understood, may make as much difference to mankind as the departure from animism as explanation of phenomena has made. We see now that we make our environment, to a degree, where formerly we thought of ourselves as mere receptors of what is already in our surroundings.

The relatively recent discoveries in the area of cooperation give us a scientific basis for a way of life which promises to enable people to live together on an altogether different plane from that which we have known. It should make a great deal of difference when we come to know that enhancement of others is a basic law of life, scientifically sound and therefore necessary, rather than being contrary to our natures, as has been commonly believed.

The notion of totality, the wholeness of man, will open doors to us. Freedom from unrealistic dualities, such as body versus mind, should free us to act differently from what we have previously been able to do. This concept has already invaded medicine, to the great benefit of those who are not in good health.

These examples are illustrations only of many scientific facts which can alter human affairs. More time will be needed for this change than is required in the world of external things. If the benefits of these new discoveries are to be enjoyed, people must change within themselves. It is much easier to make a new tool, to modify steel or wire, than it is to modify one's own self. That is why human relations lag so far behind present knowing, while manufacturing is up to the very last minute.

Part II, then, is an effort to state some practices in teaching which are indicated by modern research. It is an effort to take the data we now have and project them into action. If these facts are true, what does it mean to us as we plan educative experiences? What doors are now open to us which have formerly been closed? Abstract notions must take form in action before they attain significance. New facts call for new doing, and new facts take tenable action out of the realm of opinion. When we come into possession of new knowing, we are no longer free to hold opinions contrary to that knowing.

This is not the old progressive versus traditional argument. The old duality of progressive versus conservative is no longer useful. We are all progressive, in that we all want progress. We differ as to what will bring progress. We are all conservative, in that we all want to conserve. We see differently as to the best way to conserve. Certainly one charge upon education is to conserve human beings and human values. Any practice which wastes present or potential human resources would doubtless be condemned by all. John Dewey wrote recently: "It is a matter not of 'progressive' education but of education itself—in which the belated revolution that will enable mankind to realize on the potentials of the industrial and political revolutions has still to take place."

The crucial difference between educators is on the basis of the scientific method versus the animistic. Those who derive their teaching method from what is now known about the human organism would be in the former group. Those who get their methods from customs, habits, and traditions which cannot presently be supported from data belong to the latter group. And this is a matter of degree, since it is likely that none of us is completely free from the power of tradition or superstition.

It is best, however, for us not to try to classify people, or indulge in practices which divide us. Let us look at what is now known, and attempt to devise methods in keeping with it. Let us not cling to methods which come to us from a day when these facts were not known.

To the degree that Part II is philosophy, we hope that it is in keeping with the ideas on this matter discussed in Chapter 1. It may be said that we argue beyond the data, but we feel that that is what data are for and that data are never useful until they are argued beyond. When the philosopher comes into possession of new knowledge, it is his function to project the meaning of this knowledge in practice. The real difficulty is with those who practice in disregard of data and those who have data but do not project them in their meaning for action.

PART TWO

CHAPTER 7

Growth

The teacher who walks in the shadow of the temple among his followers, gives not of his wisdom but rather of his faith and his lovingness.

If he is indeed wise he does not bid you enter the house of his wisdom, but rather leads you to the threshold of your own mind.

—Kahlil Gibran

At the heart of the business of education is the phenomenon of growth. What the children in the classroom are doing is growing. The quantity of growth may be large or small, and its direction may enhance the individual or may hinder his enhancement. It may be beneficial in promoting his capacity for effective living, or it may be damaging. The dynamic of growth is present, however, in some quantity and is taking some direction. The task of the educator is to bring his power and skill to bear, to the end that this growth will be great in quantity and beneficial in quality and direction. (45)

If teachers held the concept of growth as the classroom dynamic, it would modify many of their procedures. It might change the teacher himself in regard to his own growth. He would then abandon the idea that children are receptacles, waiting to receive something which he has but they have not. He would see learning as process, and would feel himself to be in the middle of movement, with himself as primary facilitator. He would see that, if the child is to grow, he will have to start where he is, not where the teacher wants him to be, and that the child's progress will have to be measured from that point, rather than from some other teacher-determined point.

If the teacher sees learning as growth, he will realize that each individual must have a different goal of achievement. He will see that he cannot know the ultimate goal for any one of them. Knowing this, he will not need to become upset, amounting in some cases to panic, when all do not achieve the same goal.

THE NATURE OF GROWTH

We have long held a superficial concept of growth, which we now see will not suffice to explain what we observe. It is a commonly held notion that children grow until they get their growth, and that is the end of it. This is true in the physical sense, but since we now know that the physical body is only part of the total organism we can see that we have been looking at only part of the growth process. Functionally physical growth may be a minor part, since an organism is what it does, and what it does is largely determined by attitude, habit, knowledge, and by other factors not too closely related to over-all physical structure. When we think of the total organism as a functioning whole, it is not possible to say that one part is more important than another. But we have all seen people with fine physical structures who have grown in no other way, and have observed their incapacity to meet the emerging problems of life. We can only say that, while a good body is essential to a full and effective life, it is only part of the requirement; total growth is essential. (46)

Being habituated to observe physical growth, we have thought of it on a time-line basis. An organism should have grown so much in so many years. Such norms have some validity for physical growth, but none for total growth if individual differences are taken into account. When we consider growth in ability to think critically, or in changed attitude, we see that tremendous growth can sometimes occur in a short time or little in a long time. We cannot be too sure when great growth will take place, nor what, in individual cases, will bring it about. Much is often little, and little, much. The time-line idea has little validity.

If physical growth were all there is to it, we would have bad news for all adults, because there comes a time, somewhere between sixteen and twenty-five years of age, when the physical plant is completed and needs only to be maintained. If physical growth were the whole of it, the young adult would have little to look forward to for the most of his life. With the idea of growth for the total organism, we can see that many aspects of the total individual are only beginning, or have not even appeared, when the physical growth mercifully stops. We know now that adults grow in important aspects throughout life. An individual can change and keep on changing as long as he lives. When this dynamic ceases, death of the total organism ensues.

The notion of growth as a continuous dynamic throughout life gives hope and meaning to the whole of life. When the individual sees himself as never completed, always open to functional modification and improvement, he sees point and purpose in continued existence. (47)

The Stuffs of Growth

What does the organism need to take in from outside himself in order to grow?

There are two kinds of stuff, entirely different in nature and purpose, which the organism requires. The first of these is food and air. Materials—solid, liquid, and gas—are needed for the building of the cells which constitute the physical plant. This plant, in good condition, is essential to the total self, but it is built differently from the rest of the functioning organism.

Proper food and sufficient oxygen bring about great bodily changes, particularly in the early stages of the development of the whole. A normal infant doubles its size in six months. Once built, the structure still requires these same materials for maintenance. Throughout life these stuffs must be had to supply that which can be converted into energy and to replace worn-out cells. Since the organism is an embodiment of energy, it is the replenishment of energy through intake of convertible materials that constitutes maintenance. The body has to be equipped to sort out that which can be converted, and to eliminate the rest, since not all of these materials are appropriate.

With regard to the matter of appropriateness, readiness is a factor in all that the organism takes from the outside. Not all which an organism will need is appropriate at a special time. We do not give corned beef and cabbage to newborn babes. In most cases, the organism develops to the point where it can use these foods, but in some individual cases readiness for these viands never occurs. They are universally inappropriate in the beginning of life and selectively inappropriate throughout life. The organism cannot use any outside stuff until it is ready for it, and in some cases the organism never gets ready.

The second kind of intake for growth is perceptive stuff. This is what comes into consciousness as the result of the impingement of stimuli from outside the organism upon its receptor devices. (48)

We have not always recognized the fact that perceptive stuff builds structure as truly as does food. It surely does, however, if we remember that an organism is what it does, and that the actions of the physical plant depend upon what has been built from perception. Regardless of the degree of perfection of the physical structure, the success of the organism depends upon what has been built into structure through experience. Perception is the phenomenon that makes meaningful experience possible.

The functioning parts, which are built of perceptive stuff, are primarily attitude, habit, and knowledge. These control the physical plant, and are the basis for behavior. New experiences made possible through perception can modify attitude, habit, and knowledge so that they function differently. The possibility of modification of these controlling structures is what makes growth possible throughout life. Attitude and habit are sometimes so strongly built that they are hard to change, but there is none so strong that it will not yield to certain perceptive experiences. (49)

The perceptive stuff that is taken in is what releases energy for action. Energy is built out of foodstuffs, but the energy has no place to go until the way is pointed out and the path through which it can flow is indicated.

The essentials for perceptual intake are experience and purpose. The organism will often take in food and drink which it cannot use and may have to cast out. But our perceptual mechanism is involuntary, and therefore avoids this necessity. The organism simply does not receive through perception that which it has not experience or purpose to receive.

While we may put any old thing in our stomachs, or in the stomachs of others, the body simply refuses to receive perceptual material which it cannot use. When the organism lacks experience and purpose to receive, it lacks readiness. Now we can see more clearly how crucial to education the matter of readiness is. We have said before, and for a long time, that we cannot teach anything until the learner is ready to learn it. The force of this idea is much greater when we realize that readiness is basic to the nature of the perceptual process, and lack of readiness is not a matter of unwillingness to learn, of whim, or of fancy. When this fact is more generally recognized, we will be freed from our present feeling of obligation to perform the impossible. If the energy spent by teachers and learners in attempting to defy the factor of readiness could be turned into constructive channels, great progress in growth could be made, and readiness itself could in many cases be acquired.

He who said "He who has ears to hear, let him hear" was not talking about that which flaps in the wind. He referred to that which is between the ears. He was voicing the great truth that you cannot tell anyone anything until he has something to hear it with.

Knowledge also is a factor in what may or may not be perceived, for it is one of the residues of experience. It is mustered to help in the achievement of growth. While present knowledge is a product of growth, it is mustered to achieve new growth and to acquire new knowledge. It becomes a tool for further growth in a continuous process of mustering and acquiring. It is one of the products, but not the only one, of experience and of learning. (50)

The larger part of what an individual is functionally is built out of perceptual stuff. This part of growth is large also because it extends throughout life. The organism seeks out of its externality that which it can use. This seeking is controlled by unique purpose. The dynamic of growth, at least that which is built out of perception, is purpose.

Purpose not only controls what can come into consciousness and be built into structure, but it also points the path along which the energy that constitutes the total organism can be spent. The growth that can take place as an individual interacts with his environment, and the way in which the accumulation of power can be used depends upon the individual's purpose. (51)

Because of the uniqueness of individual purpose, the individual views whatever he takes in from the standpoint of his own enhancement or defense. Since perception is highly selective (we perceive only a few of the thousands of coincidences in our environment at any one time) and is controlled largely by purpose, it is likely that most of the things perceived are on the basis of what any particular item means to the perceiver, either to his advantage or to his danger. The purpose to enhance is ever present in the individual, and the concomitant of that enhancement is defense or protection. Since this purpose to enhance or defend is ever present and automatic, we automatically place value judgments on what we perceive. These judgments are in terms of what the situation means to the perceiver—whether it is seen as a good or as a danger.

All behavior is logical to the behaver. Certain behavior may not turn out to the ultimate advantage of the behaver. It may indeed result in his destruction. But in the light of his purpose and his interpretation of his environment, the behavior seems logical to him.

Because of the large part perception and experience play in the building of the functioning organism, they are all closely related to the growth process. These facts serve to show many limitations to the growth process. It is futile and wasteful to try to operate in opposition to them. The recognition of the part played by readiness enables us to save our energy and reveals great potentialities when we are willing to work in accord with the dynamic of growth. If we can once see that each individual has a unique purpose and that there is a path through which his energies can be spent, we will be able to facilitate growth as we have never done before. (52)

Since education and learning are growth, the question as to the role and function of the teacher naturally arises. What can a teacher do to facilitate growth; what practices seem likely to have no bearing on growth; or to stultify it?

Much of the baggage of pedagogy inherited from the dim past will have to be abandoned. For example, we will have to stop foisting subject matter upon learners because we think it is good for them. We will need to begin consultation with learners as to what is to be done, in order to take advantage of the individual paths of energy pointed out by individual purpose. We will have to abandon animism in our attitudes toward what is to be taught, and cease to use certain items of subject matter for magical reasons. We will need to cease using repudiated faculty psychology as explanation for doing what we want to do for other reasons. We will need to approach our problems with a fresh point of view, taking into account what we now know. These problems will have to be met with pioneer courage, free from the abject fear that grips so many of us when we depart from what we have held to be "tried and true." We will have to make these changes a step at a time, as we can see what we ourselves feel we can do and retain our confidence and sense of security.

Teachers cannot modify their methods and behavior by fiat any more than can learners. But teachers, along with all others, have the capacity to grow and to change in the light of new knowledge and experience. We well know that nobody is going to modify his behavior just because we tell him to do so. But as each individual teacher sees what he can do, and the reasons for doing it, new ways which are more tenable for both teacher and learner can evolve.

What the teacher has to work with in facilitating growth is primarily the perceptive stuff of growth. It is true that it sometimes becomes the function of the teacher to see to it that the student has a good meal with which to build body and to produce energy. But mostly the teacher deals with that part of growth which builds attitude, habit, and knowledge. This part of growth is the most important and most continuous and therefore the teacher's work can never be done. (53)

The analogy of the teacher's work to that of the gardener or farmer seems a good one, although the teacher's task is much more difficult because he has to work with intangibles in promoting growth out of perceptual stuff, while the gardener works with more material things. The gardener makes all possible arrangements for the growth of his plants. He places them in as advantageous a physical setting as possible; he furnishes as good soil as he can get, and supplies fertilizer and water. To a degree, he is even able to control temperature. But he never once assumes that he is going to do the growing for the plants. They will have to do that.

Similarly, the teacher makes all possible arrangements for growth to take place, but in the final analysis he has to admit that the learner must himself do the growing and that he must do it in his own way. The teacher comes to the realization that he does not teach, but that the pupil learns.

The role of the teacher, then, is one of facilitating growth. He is the stage manager and scene shifter; he provides the suitable situation for growth to take place.

He introduces value judgments as to the quality of some experiences. All experience is not educative, since some may not enhance the individual for effective living. The teacher must realize that sometimes the learner has to go through unprofitable experiences because he cannot at the moment accept the idea that the experience he wants is not enhancing. Patience during unprofitable experiences is only part of the teacher's art in leading the learner to more profitable experiences. It is in the nature of a detour on the way to goals which will ultimately enhance the learner. The teacher's aim is to rearray the body of experience in such a way that it will be usable to the learner and constructive in its total quality.

The teacher has another role besides the one of facilitator. This is his role as resource person. He is the oldest and most experienced person in the group. He knows facts which can contribute to the growth of the learner, and can short-cut the learner's work. The teacher does not need to withhold products of his own experience on the theory that it is good for the learner to acquire it the hard way. All possible short cuts and facilitation will make for just that much more growth, for an answer properly provided leads to further questions. When a learner becomes invested with known anwers, he can use them as tools for finding unknown answers.

When the teacher serves as a resource person, when supplying an answer seems to be called for, he must avoid the implication of finality, or the pose of an authority. He must keep himself in the middle of a free-flowing, changing situation. The role of authority delimits learning and is untenable. Such a role will lead the teacher into demanding staticity because the group's activities will have to be geared to what the teacher knows. The teacher needs to make it clear at all times that, while his longer life has given him some answers to which the learners are welcome, he does not know everything, and is himself in a learning and growing situation. Thus can he avoid becoming geared to the static in a world of change. Known answers, while useful to further knowing, are the smaller part of life. As the learners leave school and become integrated into social life, they will live much more in a situation of change than of staticity.

* * * *

Growth is the crucial activity of the learning process. That part of growth which uses perceptual stuff is continuous throughout life. The task of the teacher is to facilitate growth, particularly in the areas of attitude, habit, and knowledge. The chapters that follow will have to do with ways and means of bringing about this growth.

CHAPTER 8

Communication

". . . the patriotic Archbishop of Canterbury, found it advisable—"
"Found *what?*" said the Duck.
"Found it," the Mouse replied, rather crossly: "Of course you know what 'it' means."
"I know what 'it' means well enough, when I find something," said the Duck: "It's generally a frog, or a worm."

—Lewis Carroll

We can see now that one of the crucial and difficult problems of human life is communication between people. This is the process by which one human being can to a degree know what another thinks, feels, or believes. It is the means by which an individual's need for others can be satisfied. It is the source of all growth except body building, and the key to human relatedness. Communication is not so easy as has been assumed. We have assumed that if we told another something, he knew it; if we showed him something, he saw it. We now know that nothing could be more uncertain or unreliable.

The organism faces a dilemma. Perception is the avenue through which all growth except the physical must come. Because of the nature of perception, no two individuals can have precisely the same perception or make the same use of it. We have no given common world with any other being, but only the possibility of achieving one to a degree through improved communication.

While the organism has no common given world with any other, it has powerful social needs. It needs other human beings, and it cannot survive and flourish without them. Since we have no given common world and since communication is difficult, the easy way

78

would seem to be to go it alone. Many people try this, but they grow in inhuman ways, and become less and less adequate and successful as human beings. The dilemma lies in our uniqueness, and our need for others.

Added to the difficulty of communication is the need that we have to build invisible barriers between ourselves and others. The individual's primary objective is self-enhancement. An automatic concomitant of enhancement is defense. We put value judgments on what we perceive, as to whether it promises us weal or woe. We attempt to defend ourselves by not letting others get too close to us. We do this because we all know at least some of our own weaknesses, and know that we are not so invulnerable as we hope others will think we are. If we are to enhance ourselves, part of the process involves concealing our weak spots. We therefore conduct ourselves so that others will not be able to know too much about our inner selves. Some have built their barriers so thick and high that they are all defense. Words simply bounce off such exteriors, and these individuals are deprived of the stuff of growth.

These barriers we believe to be automatic and inescapable, although they exist in varying degrees. They can be reduced by experiences which give confidence in other human beings. The people who feel the least need for the protection of barriers are the ones who can enhance themselves the most. They are the ones who can best take advantage of the rich possibilities for growth made possible by communion with others. They can live most fully because they can meet the social requirements of adequate human life.

The importance, and the difficulty, of communication between individuals thus become apparent, for communication is the means by which we can know about others. It is the way by which the perceptive stuff of growth, which controls attitude, knowledge, and behavior, can be acquired. It is through communication that the basic loneliness of the self can at least to a degree be overcome and that hunger for the others may be assuaged. (54)

The business of teaching is communication. This does not mean that the communication needs to be all from the teacher to the student. It may be from student to teacher, or it may be between students. But the teacher's stock in trade is the perceptive stuff of growth, whatever the source and whoever the receiver. The teacher who can facilitate communication will promote growth, although we ignore for the moment the quality and direction of this growth. The teacher who blocks communication will stunt growth and will build barriers. If we could all look upon the task of teaching as one of facilitating qualitative communication between teacher and learner as well as among learners, teachers would behave differently from their present common practice.

The most important method of communication that we have is language. This is an accomplishment which seems to be peculiarly human. It is possible because of the capacity of the human organism to entertain abstractions. Sounds are made to have meanings which, to a degree, are commonly held. These sounds are further abstracted so that they can be represented by writing; thus we have the use not only of the spoken word but of the written word as well.

There is no space here to trace the development and significance of language. That has been done by competent scholars. The semanticists, particularly the International Society for General Semantics, have performed an outstanding service in increasing our understanding of the nature, uses, and weaknesses of language.

We now know that, while language is our most useful and universal method of communication, it is not the perfect instrument that we have held it to be. We know this partly through the work of the semanticists and partly through our more recent understanding of the perceptive process. Words do not have the precise meaning we have assumed they had because they are themselves changing and evolving and because they have to be subjectively interpreted by the receiver and are always interpreted in the light of the receiver's unique experience, purpose, and value system. Besides, words have an affective value, related to emotions rather than to abstract meaning, and this affective value is also unique and unpredictable. (55)

Illustrations of misinterpretation of words on the basis of experience are common. Our lore is full of stories similar to the one about the "consecrated cross-eyed bear." When this type of humor emerges in a group, almost everyone has a story to tell which illustrates this fact. The significance of such misinterpretation, however, seems lost in many cases, especially among teachers who still think that what they say should be heard and understood exactly as they mean it.

Because of this variation in interpretation, or extracted meaning, it can be seen that two-way communication through language is much more efficient than is one-way communication. Two-way communication takes place most commonly (though not alone) in using the spoken language. In conversation or in discussion groups it is possible to ask for clarification, to get the speaker to say it another way, or for restatement by the receiver.

Two-way communication is possible but not common in the written word. Perhaps it occurs most often in correspondence, where it is possible to ask for clarification. One-way communication is possible in the spoken word, and indeed often occurs, as in lectures, and in "telling people off." Even when a conversation is taking place, the communication may be one-way, because, while one is speaking, the listener may be thinking of what he is going to say when the other has finished. We have all been in gatherings where everyone is talking and nobody is listening, with the result that not even one-way communication is occurring. Language is indeed capable of many vagaries.

The written word is a tool of enormous usefulness to the human race. Through it, it is possible to receive communication from those who are separated from us in space and time. In its limited way, it is thus an eliminator of space and time. We are able to receive not only from those who are removed from us geographically, but also from those who have long since died. The written word is the only means by which we may know the thoughts and contributions of all those who have gone before. It is also time-binding, as the semanticists have pointed out, so that we may to a degree take ourselves out of the time in which we live and bind ourselves to the time of the writer.

We need to recognize, however, that as an instrument of communication the written word has some inherent weaknesses which reduce its effectiveness as a tool. It is almost always one-way communication. There is ordinarily no opportunity to question the writer as to his exact meaning. Since language is ever evolving, the meanings of a writer far removed from us in time or space may be quite different from those attributed to him by us. (56)

We use the written word for such fundamental things as constitutions and contracts. But we have to maintain an elaborate court system chiefly for the purpose of deciding what the words in these documents really mean in our time. It is the present interpretation that functions in action. Thus our national constitution, assumed to be the unchanging rock on which our national life is built, changes every time the Supreme Court hands down a decision. The constitution is not what the founding fathers wrote, but what current judges say it is. This is a great good, because it makes possible, to a degree, the evolution of the constitution as a foundation for a changing world.

Most of the writing that we read, however, has no court for interpretation except the reader. He does his own interpreting in the light of his own unique experience and purpose. These interpretations not only vary from the meaning of the writer, but also between individual contemporary readers. When it is necessary to have a court with a judge, twelve jurors, and at least two lawyers to decide what was meant by a contract written recently in careful legal language, we are led to wonder how accurate is the interpretation of the solitary subjective reader who is attempting to receive communication from words written long ago by people he has never seen. (57)

The written word is a useful tool, but an inadequate one if understanding and communion are to be achieved. Its greatest service, perhaps, is in literature, where the reader is expected to make his own interpretation, as he does in participating with the artist in any form of art. In graphic art, sculpture, music, and literature, the precise meaning of the artist is unimportant; what his art means to the observer is the main thing. Words as literature have affective value for readers, and in the case of great literature continue to have such value through the ages. Written words are much more useful in this function than they are in the conveying of so-called facts. In handing down the culture and experience of the race, it is likely that even this is more accurately conveyed in literature, through the affective value of words, than in factual records.

The use of language, spoken and written, is our most common way of communicating between individuals. It is by no means the only way. In fact, some of the other media may convey deeper feeling and understanding than is possible with language. Group dancing and group singing are two ways by which feeling can be conveyed without language. Bodily contact with another, however slight, may carry much meaning. Sometimes more can be told by a touch of the hand than by any amount of speaking. Much that we are and want others to know lies deep within us as total organisms, and we cannot bring it to the surface for verbalization.

Mutual experiencing of arts of all kinds may bring people together. We have mentioned great literature. People who listen to great music together or who view paintings, ceramics, or sculpture often are drawn together by mutual affective experiences.

All these methods of communication involve other people; they are two-way. They consist of two or more people doing something together. The most effective communication occurs when people do things together toward the achievement of a commonly accepted goal. It is then that we come to know each other so well that, while we still make subjective interpretations, we can say that we achieve a considerable degree of communion. It is in this way that we can overcome the lack of a given common world, and to a great degree can achieve one. Here we see the significance of the statement that we have no *given* common world but that we can *achieve* one through common action. Mutual enterprise toward commonly held goals, then, is not just a recommended, pleasant frill. It is the means by which the social demands of the organism may be met.

Teaching is the business of communication in all its forms. To get knowledge, feeling, attitude, understanding from one human being to another is what schools are for. The more we make use of what we know about communication the more effective teaching and learning will be.

If communication is to be effective, the first thing we must do is to reduce the barriers between teacher and learner, and between learner and learner. If we could see these barriers as we can see barbed-wire fences we would immediately understand that they are preventing movement, and we would tear them away. (58)

Teachers often unwittingly increase rather than decrease barriers. They act to increase their status, so that they will be further removed from those with whom they must exchange. Every act which tends to put the teacher on a pedestal tends to establish distance and barriers between teacher and learner, and thus makes the possibility of communication more difficult and unlikely.

Teachers everywhere work under a handicap in this regard. We have inherited status from the past which is difficult to overcome. It is not alone status which separates us from our students, but a feeling on their part that we are not to be trusted, that we are basically dishonest. This can come only from the experiences students have had with teachers who *were* dishonest. When the teacher tries to establish with his students the confidence that is essential to operation, they often refuse to believe that the teacher will not "double-cross" them. They feel sure he will "spring" an examination which lies outside their agreements, and that it will contain trick questions designed to catch them.

This is a heritage which all teachers who would live productively with their students must carry. It exists because, for centuries, many teachers have been bad actors. They have erred in two major ways.

One is that they have tried to build status for themselves by aloofness and mystery. They have done this, we believe, because they have felt the need to build defenses against their own weaknesses. They have posed as authorities on subject matter when they knew they were not authorities. In order to prevent their students from discovering that their pose as authorities was a sham, they have tried to build distance between themselves and their students. They have done such things as trying to confine learning to what was in the textbook and to material presented by them in lectures.

The other error is even more reprehensible. Teachers have tricked their students by the evaluative devices they have used. They have contrived examinations designed not to give a true picture of the student's learning but to try to find something which the student did not know, or to put the question in such a way that the student would misunderstand it. These acts tended to build stronger the barriers between teacher and student, and to reduce the possibility of communication to a trickle. Such acts may be good in defending the teacher's inadequate ego, or in maintaining his prestige as an authority, if that were the objective of the school.

Since spoken and written words are such important tools in the classroom, great care needs to be taken to see that the gift of language is used to full advantage. In using language, the teacher needs to be sure that his words are within the experience of the learner. Adults have a difficult problem in keeping their vocabularies within the word range of children with whom they would communicate. Using words because we like them and understand them has nothing to do with the case; words must also be understood by the person to whom they are directed. We know one teacher who boasts that he deliberately talks so that not more than 10 per cent of his students can understand him. He says he is raising horizons, but he is really causing 90 per cent of his students to look at the floor, unaware of any glories on the horizon. Communication here is foredoomed. Perhaps this teacher should raise the standards of his vocabulary and concepts just a little higher, so that nobody would understand him. He would then be perfect in his effort to block communication. There is a chance that he is more interested, basically, in raising his own status than in "raising horizons."

The written words we use also need to be within the scope and understanding of the reader. Because the written word has assumed such overwhelming importance in our educational procedures, we are anxious (too anxious) for all students to be good and avid readers. Reading has become a good in itself, instead of a useful tool.

If a child is to become a good reader, he must have an opportunity to read material which he is able to read. Learning feeds on learning, and the progress of upgrading will take place if the student reads. Teachers of young children who are just learning to read do try to have the reading material within the understanding of the child, although many crimes have been committed by the deadly dullness of the "Pat-has-a-cat" type of stuff. In the higher grades the worst offenders are the lecturers and the literature teachers. We try to thrust literary work down the throats of children when the words involved are completely devoid of meaning. We know a teacher who is ready to die for *A Tale of Two Cities*. Most of her students do not care about it and cannot understand it; the net result is that they develop an aversion to it, to

Charles Dickens, and to literary works in general. *A Tale of Two Cities* is a fine literary work if used right, and both the work and the author deserve better treatment.

Literature teachers err also, we believe, when they pick literature apart and spend hours on what the author meant by each passage. As has been pointed out, a literary work is a work of art, and needs to be taken in as a whole. Analysis is destructive of the wholeness of the work, and of the affective value contemplated by the author. When affective value goes out, boredom sets in, and the effect is to destroy the very values we seek to establish.

The lecture, designed presumably to communicate from teacher to learner, is used in our educational system far out of proportion to its value. This is not to say that the lecture method never should be employed. It has its place, but if it is viewed as a tool of communication, one can readily see that it has great weaknesses, that it often, if not usually, fails to convey meaning. Therefore, it should be used only when it serves. In any ordinary school situation the lecture method does not need to be used; other ways of communicating can be devised which will accomplish more.

We are justified in using any device which does not violate the dignity of other human beings, provided we know why we are using it, what we may hope to accomplish by it, and what the adverse factors are. We should recognize, then, that the lecture is strictly one-way communication. This means that the words may or may not be received by the supposed listeners. In many cases we know that they will not be received at all because there is no involvement of the other, the listener. When a person is not involved in what is going on around him, his attention is likely to slip away, whether he wants to listen or not. In many cases the listener deliberately turns his attention to other matters, either because he is not interested in what the lecturer says or because he resents the lack of participation.

Assuming that the words are actually received by the listener, that they have not bounced off him, there still is the matter of subjective interpretation of the words received. The words will not mean the same to the listener as they do to the lecturer, and the transfer of meaning will be thwarted to a degree. Because the lecture is one-way, there is no opportunity for clarification or involvement. (59)

In the light of what is known about perception, learning, and the significance of doing and involvement, we are forced to question the value of one-way spoken communication. Its best use would seem to be when large audiences are involved, and where the purpose of the lecture is to produce an affective value rather than a rational one. The lecturer then needs to be something of a showman. Even then we question whether the affective value is often translated into behavior. If preaching could save the world, it should have been saved long ago, when we consider the amount of preaching that has gone on in schools and churches in our long history. The fact is that people do not ordinarily behave better because they have been told to do so. For the most part, the people in our prisons are not there because they never were told how they should live. Behavior seems to be controlled more deeply than by the superficial reception of words. The process of improvement seems to be one of mutual involvement. We learn to live well by living well, not by being told to live well.

Since we are considering language as an instrument of communication, we cannot escape a consideration of the uses to which grammar is put in our educational system. Grammar is an explanation of language, a set of rules for usage. It is valuable as a guide, but it comes after usage, not before it. It is not an end in itself, nor a suitable approach to language. Children learn to talk by the time they are two years old, and by ten they usually talk well although most ten-year-olds know no grammar. The overemphasis on grammar has a tendency to interfere with, rather than facilitate, usage. Grammar is used as a good, as a disciplinary tool, to the enormous boredom of learners, and to the stultification of language as a means of communication. Grammar should be used sparingly, as an explanation of language which has been used, not as an approach to language.

While language could be a good tool for drawing people together, it is often used as a tool for increasing distance between people. The teacher who thinks his function is to criticize increases the distance between himself and his students. When learners are criticized concerning their use of language, their natural reaction is to decide to keep still in the future. Criticism can be constructive and helpful, but it is a dangerous tool which has to be used skillfully and sparingly, if at all. When a teacher acts in such a manner that he reduces the flow of language he ruins his best tool for communication. He renders useless his chief stock in trade.

The use of sarcasm and ridicule serves to dam up the flow of ideas. These "low" devices are used to make the learner feel small, so that the teacher, without growing himself, will feel big. They satisfy the egoistic drives of the teacher to the detriment of the learner. They never serve any good purpose. Even the satisfaction felt by the teacher is bogus, and his seeming growth will not serve him when he needs it.

On the same low level is the predilection of teachers to use "bawling out" as a device. We get satisfaction from "telling people off," but it is doubtful if this device ever did any receiver any good, although it may temporarily have relieved the aggressive feelings of the sender. When a teacher uses this device, it would be good if he could realize that he is the one who is getting the therapy, such as it is, and that the learner is being driven farther and farther from him, so that real communication resulting in learning and in growth becomes more and more difficult.

In order that communication and learning may be at their best, all the means must be freely in action. Since language is so important, there should be much of it, spoken and written. The way to learn to speak and to write is to speak and to write, freely, in quantity, without fear. The more one talks and writes the better one will do so. Such quantity of usage can be promoted only in an atmosphere of confidence—confidence that the spoken words will be received sympathetically and that written words will be read in the same spirit. The objective of writing is that someone will read. The teacher who requires papers which he does not read cuts off his end of the communication and takes the purpose out of the writing.

Important as language is in communication, we need to re-examine its strengths and weaknesses, and what we may expect of it. Language has become an end rather than a means in our classrooms. Reading, writing, lecturing, and grammar have been elevated beyond what we can sensibly expect from them. The gardener has come to admire the hoe rather than the flowers and vegetables. We need to re-examine the tool to see what it is good for, and how its uses may be improved, remembering always that it is a means, not an end. (60)

In discussing communication we have perhaps spent too much space on language. That is because it is overemphasized in education, and we need to take a good look at it, to see whether, as used, it is actually increasing communion and learning, or whether its misuse is decreasing and delimiting growth.

If learning and communication are to be at their best, there must be much doing together, so that all the ways by which understandings are conveyed will come into use. The deeper meanings that we need so much to contribute to each other come, it seems, through comradeship in working at a mutual enterprise. The doing in common seems to effect deeper changes than do words and these changes modify people so that they behave differently. Such fellowship is the ultimate that we know in the modification of human beings in the direction of making them more human.

CHAPTER 9

Cooperation

'What is the nature of life?' can be expressed in one word, co-operation—the interaction between organisms for mutual support in such a way as to confer survival benefits upon each other. Another word for the same thing is love. Without co-operation, without love, it is not possible to live—at best, it is possible only to exist.

—Ashley Montagu

In Chapter 4 we have discussed the fact that the basic method of progress for all living things is cooperation. Advance in complexity of organisms became possible only when cells began to cling together. If this clinging together had not occurred, all life would still be single-celled.

Another all-important event occurred when cells began to aggregate. They began to specialize. Certain cells took over special tasks which they performed for the whole. Some cells were better adapted to certain tasks than others. This specialization made it possible for clusters of cells to become organisms. Without specialization, there would be only clusters of cells, each cell carrying out, in a meager way, all the functions of life. There would have been no advancement in organization. The cells themselves might have been worse off than they had been separately, because their opportunities for securing food and oxygen would have been reduced. (61)

The opportunity to specialize, to perform separate functions better than any one cell could do them all and to perform these functions for others while others were doing different tasks for them, is the basis for all living tissue or organism above the level of the single cell. And so it is when people do things together.

90

Their uniqueness is what gives individuals value in social organization. If people were all alike, had the same abilities, there would be little value in association. None could learn from others; none could perform tasks which others could not do for themselves.

Uniqueness, then, is perhaps man's greatest asset, since it gives him something to give, something to do, and something to learn from others. It is what gives him his place, gives him value and worth. Uniqueness, therefore, needs to be cherished and fostered. Difference in abilities, in experience, and in purpose needs to be seen as the quality that makes the individual precious to the welfare of all. (62)

What has been said about the importance of communication leads us directly to a discussion of cooperation. If people are to communicate, they must get together; the organism's social demands require it. Besides getting together, they need to do things together, for in doing together all the avenues of communication are brought into use. There will be no lengthy discussion here of what cooperation is, its elements or techniques, because that has often been done by others and does not need to be repeated here. We have discussed the scientific basis for it in Part I.

There is, however, one element in the cooperative process which needs attention. That is the fact that the process itself seems to have therapeutic value for the individuals involved. We do not presently know so much about this as we should like and perhaps will know in time. We have, however, observed this therapeutic phenomenon on many occasions: As people work together they seem to change in the direction of being more energetic, more understanding, more human. This change does not seem to be related to the personal qualities of the people worked with, nor to the level of the group goal. It seems not to be a purely intellectual change, but to involve the whole organism. It is not often possible for the person who has undergone this change to verbalize it at all. He behaves differently, however, and since the change is not a superficial acquisition, he continues to behave differently. It may be that the finding of an outlet for the expenditure of energy in accordance with unique purpose accounts for this change and the apparent depth of it. (63)

The cooperative process is, therefore, the best means, perhaps the only means, known to us whereby people are themselves fundamentally changed in the direction of being more human so that they act more humanly. People accustomed to behavior which does not promote the welfare of others will not cease this behavior by being told that it is unwise or immoral or because they are punished for it. In order to change behavior, the organism itself must be changed. This can best be done by giving the individual an opportunity to experience gratifying release of the energy of which he is constituted. (64)

Competition is the opposite of cooperation in human behavior. Since cooperation is a good and, as we know now, a requirement for human growth, competition is an evil. The terms "good" and "evil" are used simply on the basis of what facilitates human growth as against what hinders it. The human being is a social being, or he is nothing. Cooperation brings people together, providing the means and the setting for human intercourse. Competition drives people apart, rendering intercourse difficult or impossible. (65)

In the early stages of an individual's life, competition, while not natural in the sense that it comes from nature, is inherent in the situation. The organism has its own ego to enhance and to defend. The naïve approach to this enhancement and defense is simply to take what one wants—to demand the center of attention, whether it affects others adversely or not. The child is able to take this approach long before he can entertain ethical concepts or can have judgment as to the over-all significance of his conduct. He cannot at this stage be expected to see that his own enhancement is related to the enhancement of others. Perhaps the reason why cells and other lower forms of life are able to aggregate to mutual advantage more readily than human beings can is that cells do not have egoistic drives to contend with. They are not able to think, and so they cannot think on a low level, as human beings can. (66)

There are other evils which are more or less inherent in the situation in which the young child finds himself. One of these is stealing—taking the possessions of others. Long before the child can have any sense of the rights of others to keep their possessions he becomes large enough physically to carry the property of others away. Normally he comes to see that such acts make his own possessions insecure, and that the system where each helps himself will not work. Later still he may come to realize that what helps others helps him. So he tends to overcome the impulse to take the property of others, which originally seemed such a natural and logical solution to his desires.

Lying is an evil which comes in the same category. The child learns to talk long before he can possibly comprehend the significance of telling the truth. He comes into possession of the wonderful tool of language, and at his age he cannot see any reason why he should not use it for what seems to him to be his advantage. As he grows older he learns that if he misuses this tool he dulls it. Language is no good for communication unless the person to whom it is directed believes what is said. Thus the child learns that this misuse of language ends in the weakening of language for effective purposes. He has to establish a reputation for truthfulness among those with whom he would communicate, or for reliability in the use of language. The old story of the boy who cried "Wolf!" too many times illustrates a sad outcome for one who ruined the effectiveness of this tool of communication. (67)

It is a curious aspect of our society that, while lying and stealing are recognized as evils and are strongly inhibited, competition, perhaps more damaging than lying or stealing, is encouraged. In fact, too much is done too early to inhibit lying and stealing, before the child can have the ethical concepts that make this inhibition sensible to him. And pretty generally in our culture stealing is regarded as more reprehensible than lying. We are indeed touched when property values are at stake. Lying and stealing would in many cases inhibit themselves if given time, because they are impractical.

If it were left to itself, competition also would inhibit itself as impractical, but we not only encourage it as a good but we put children in positions where they have no choice but to resort to it. If we left him alone, it would become apparent to any individual that he would be better off with the help of others and that help is a mutual transaction. The powerful need each has for others, if given any kind of chance at all, would drive them together for the satisfaction of mutual social hunger.

Competition is an evil because it drives people apart and causes them to grow in twisted forms. It is a denial of the need of each for other. Without the satisfaction of this need, no organism can grow in the direction of human fulfillment. Competition is untenable because it drives the individual too hard, and deprives him of his full equipment of satisfied social need. Our tenuous mental balance and our tissues so completely related cannot take it. So people often die in what should be the fullness of life because their total organisms find the task of life impossible and give up the struggle.

The question will arise as to whether all competition is evil. Is it damaging for children to run races, or to play a game of baseball, or for people to bowl or to play bridge?

Game activities not only are not harmful but may be beneficial provided that the game is played for the sake of the game and that the pleasure of winning is intrinsic in the game itself. Because we all have egoistic drives for self-enhancement, and because life has many frustrations, we are inclined to develop feelings of aggression which need some wholesome outlet. Bowling is particularly good for such release because it involves the whole organism, and the sight of the flying pins gives such immediate results. A bridge game can provide similar values in a more sedentary way. Because it is more sedentary, it involves less of the total organism and is therefore probably less therapeutic.

The point where these activities become evil is when they are so constructed or so played as to have the damage of another as their objective. If two boys in a playground want to run a race to see which can get to a certain spot more quickly, no important damage is done to winner or to loser. Of course, if one is obviously faster than the other, the slower one will not enter the contest. Before the event can occur he has to think he has a chance to win. A cripple does not voluntarily enter a foot race.

When the "chips are down," when the damage of another is the obvious outcome, then competition, whether in games or in other phases of life, becomes an evil. At this point ethics begin to be compromised, and the greater the tempo and the stakes the less the ethics. Such a result is bound to come about because no one can be ethical unless the situation permits it. Survival comes first.

To see the difference between a game played for itself and one played for extrinsic values, we need only to observe what has happened to the game of interscholastic football. In our youth football was played for the fun of it. We bought our own uniforms if we had any, and played other schools or other town teams because we liked to do so. There were no gate receipts and almost no spectators. Even after we were out of high school we got up teams and played other similarly assembled groups. There were no eligibility rules because it was assumed that each side would assemble as good players as it could find. We enjoyed a wholesome afternoon of physical activity, and the matter as to who won was relatively unimportant.

Now intercollegiate and interscholastic football is no longer played for fun. Reputations having cash value are at stake. Downtown quarterbacks act as though they made the tackles themselves. In many cases gamblers run the teams. Coaches are in intense struggles for survival, and while they may hold theoretical standards of ethics, they cannot hold to them when survival is at stake.

College officials meet and draw up rules by which they agree to abide, but they have put themselves in positions where they are unable to abide by their written word. Stadium bonds are falling due. To fill the stadium demands a winner, for the loyal alumni who seek personal aggrandizement through the team will not buy tickets when there is much risk of being cast in the role of loser.

The officials are then forced to break their agreements by paying their athletes, or getting someone else to pay them. They have to begin cheating on admission and scholastic standards. We then have the spectacle of young men, hardly more than boys, being slipped money sub rosa by those to whom they look for moral and ethical standards.

The sad fact is that, once involved, there is no way out of the dilemma. If the officials should meet and agree to pay their athletes certain amounts, it would only raise the level (financially but not ethically) of the cheating. The officials would simply have to start paying at a higher level. Soon the level would be such that there would not be enough left to retire the bonds, even with a winner. The whole system carries the seeds of its own destruction.

There is here no intention to blame the college officials except to the degree that they made their own dilemmas. Many of them are trapped in a pernicious system which involves bonds, coaches, sports writers, alumni, and gamblers, with overlapping in the last two categories. We well remember the furor when President Hutchins of the University of Chicago found that there was no honest way for his school to continue to play football. It seemed that he had no right to decide whether or not football continue. He was taking the bread out of the mouths of sports writers and the glory out of the souls of alumni. If he had not been a rugged character, he would have been pushed out of the only position that was tenable for him.

The football disease has already extended to the secondary schools, where many of the manifestations of the college game have appeared. Now there is considerable pressure to extend interscholastic football to the elementary schools, because the boys are coming into high school unprepared to make touchdowns. There seems to be no place where a quarantine can be established.

Football seems deserving of this space because it occupies such an important place in American education and life, and because it so neatly illustrates the transition from a game that was played for fun to one that scarcely anyone but the spectators any longer enjoys. This game illustrates how, when the chips are down, competitive activity insidiously leads good people into inhuman behavior. It may even be that, in our time, the game will destroy itself and thus complete the cycle. Then boys can start playing it again, without spectators or gate receipts, because they enjoy it.

Football is not the only competitive aspect of our schools. It happens to be the most spectacular one, probably because it is an interscholastic activity and, therefore, more easily observed. The stakes are in the form of cash and thus more comprehensible to a cash-minded society. It furnishes a nice illustration because its ultimate self-destruction is already in sight.

In our classrooms children are pitted against each other in struggles which are often intense. The winners are extolled, the losers punished, to the detriment of both. It is to their detriment because it deprives each of the other, and thus defeats the human social need.

It has been noted that a cripple does not voluntarily enter a foot race. But in our classes the "cripples," those who are inept at the particular activity, are entered in the race involuntarily, although defeat is a foregone conclusion. We call these people dull because this particular undertaking is not their forte. Continuous defeat brings about discouragement and then rejection, so that what we call dullness becomes intensified. We now know that brightness and dullness are, within wide limits, the products of environment. Dullness thus is an achievement, rather than a natural state. (69)

The competitive methods of our schools, foisted upon children in contradiction of their basic natures, are defended by many who say that society outside school is bitterly competitive and that children are being prepared for the struggle ahead.

The answer to that is twofold. First, life outside school is not nearly so competitive as life in school. Our big corporations have found that they are better off if they enter into agreements with their competitors which prevent mutual destruction. There is a question as to whether this arrangement contributes to the total good, but for them it is better. Many workers are on civil service, where they are protected from the vicissitudes of raw competition. Labor has banded people together for protection, and has established seniority rights in order to protect the older from the vigor of the young. While it is true that some people are engaged in highly competitive pursuits, the school today stands as our most competitive institution. We have far outdone society in this regard.

Second, there are unfortunately many evils in the world, but it does not occur to us to educate for any of them except for competition. Our youth will encounter a world in which there is considerable lying and stealing. We educate for these inadvertently, but not intentionally. To be logical, we should be deliberately developing effective thieves and liars.

It is of course a well-known fact that under our present system much cheating does go on. This cheating is done by fine young people who, in other situations, have high ideals and high ethical standards. There is a different moral code extant when it comes to schoolwork. This difference is because these young people have been forced to operate under unethical conditions. Survival is basic. The teacher is fair game, because he places himself in the position of an inquisitor and often resorts to trick methods. Since there is a lack of rapport between teacher and student, the student sees no reason why he should not behave in accordance with the milieu in which he is involuntarily cast. Whenever a teacher discovers that his young people are cheating he needs to look to the practices that make this behavior seem logical to the behaver.

A great deal of the cheating that goes on in our schools consists of young people helping one another. This would not seem to be evil in itself, except that it must be done surreptitiously, and deceit is essential to it. It would seem that almost the worst crime that young people in school can commit is to help one another. This situation controverts one of the most basic of human drives. Further, it is limiting because it is obvious that no one can learn as much without help as he can with it. We will all learn little enough, compared to what is to be learned, if we help each other all we can.

The principal device for speeding up and intensifying the competitive nature of our education is the grading system. This is a lazy form of motivation—a device designed to get people to do something they otherwise would not do. It is too inaccurate a device really to tell anyone much about the individual. It is true that many of its evils lie in the way it is used by parents and teachers in order to intensify the competitive atmosphere of our classes. It could be de-emphasized by adults, and it does not need to do so much harm as it now does. It is man-made and can be modified by man.

Perhaps the most striking misuse of the grading system is in the application of the probability curve to small numbers. This practice is followed in order to justify the limitation of the number of top grades available, so that the competitive situation will be more intense. It ought to amuse the statisticians, who have said that if any large number of individuals are measured with regard to any quality, the results, when graphed, will form a bell-shaped curve, low at the extremes, high in the middle. The educators have not waited for the probability curve to occur, but have created it artificially. They make the people fit the curve instead of letting the curve fit the people, and no statistician ever claimed that the bell-shaped probability curve would result if applied to small numbers of individuals. It is not uncommon for us to acquire an abstraction and then try to make it fit. The abstraction then becomes the center rather than the facts from which the abstraction should be derived. (70)

While competition for grades is held by many to stimulate learning, it actually has the opposite effect. When the learner has done all he needs to do in order to get the grade he wants, he naturally quits. Some students who are adept at the tricks of the trade find it possible to get good grades with scarcely any learning at all. So the effect of the grading system is to delimit and stultify learning, to hold learning activities below the creative level, to confine what is learned to what will pay off.

The grading system also delimits learning by shifting the objective away from learning. It changes the object of the enterprise. When one is concentrating on the vagaries of the teacher and what he is likely to include in his examination, he is diverted from that which might have been learned, and is perverting his energies in the direction of ephemeral and spurious value.

The reduction of learning due to the competition for grades shows the effect of extrinsic rewards in general. The reason for doing anything should lie in the value derived from the doing. In other words, the reward should be intrinsic to the task. The reason for reading a book, for example, should be to find out what is in the book, not to get a mark in a class record. Books from which the reader cannot profit should not be read. The extrinsic reward leads alleged learners to do all kinds of inappropriate tasks. Time which could have been profitably used is wasted and genuine learning which could have been acquired goes untouched.

The customary methods of teaching, where what is to be learned is decided in advance by the teacher, fails to cherish uniqueness. This quality, which gives the individual his place and points his possibilities for service, is discouraged and diminished. Rather than cultivating uniqueness, we try to get everyone to be as much alike as possible. We even group together people who are similar so that we can make their similarities more complete. Then we give them all the same lesson and strive for the same learning. The X groups are quite proud of their Xness, but they are deprived of the special and necessary talents of the Y and Z groups. Such a practice is a denial of the basic need for cooperation, where each has a unique contribution for all. Uniqueness, communication, cooperation form the basis for human development; any practice which limits these is encouraging growth in abnormal and unhuman ways.

In the light of what we now know about the demands of the human organism we can see what types of school activities build human beings and what types do not. Many of the activities in our schools are cooperative and constructive. Most of the unwholesome practices occur in the classrooms, where habitual and mistaken notions of learning prevail.

Activities can be judged by observing whether they bring people together or drive them apart. Are the walls of isolation between people being built stronger, or reduced? Are people growing in mutual confidence so that interaction is becoming more feasible? Is communication between learners being facilitated? Are people coming to feel more secure in being themselves? Are they nearer personal peace with each other, which must come before local and international warfare can be eliminated?

Cooperation is the method by which all living things facilitate each other and themselves. It is another name for what Sinnott calls organization. It is demanded by the individual in his quest for social intercourse. It is the logical implication of uniqueness. It is a force which our schools have not yet learned to use in sufficient quantity and quality. The incorporation of cooperation in educational method sets the primary problem for teachers and learners in our time. (71)

CHAPTER 10

Freedom

The principle of individual freedom is deeply rooted in the constitution of human beings. The truth embodied in it cannot die no matter how much force is brought down upon it.

—John Dewey

The human organism, and all other organisms, continuously seeks freedom. Long before man could understand the basis for his actions, he struggled with tyranny and sought liberty. He probably knew only that he felt better when he was free than he did when he was enslaved. The struggle for freedom is one of the outstanding features of history. Right up to the present time, the greatest contending forces in our world are between those who would enslave and those who would be free. This struggle shows no sign of abatement but rather seems to grow in intensity.

We see now more clearly than before why man and other organisms behave in this way. All living things are uniquely purposive. They are bundles of energy seeking to spend themselves in keeping with their unique purposes. Purpose has no meaning in the absence of freedom. Therefore, to say that an organism is purposive is to say also that freedom is a requirement. All purposive behavior—and this means all behavior—is a search for freedom. Slavery and freedom are ways of determining how energy shall be spent. If energy is spent in accordance with unique purpose, freedom is the result. If energy is forced by outside factors to be spent contrary to purpose, slavery is suffered. (72)

We observe purposive behavior in even the very lowest forms of life. Purposive behavior in these low forms is the opportunity to choose. It occurs long before the dawn of consciousness. The search for freedom, then, is no recent phenomenon. It did not begin at Runnymede, or at Concord. These historical events were manifestations of an age-old quest which goes back to the dawn of life. (73)

Surely one of the differences between living and nonliving substance is shown here. This observation brings us no nearer to an answer to the old question "What is life?" but purposive behavior is an observable phenomenon displayed by the living. Nonliving things seem to act at times, but their freedoms and restrictions are mechanical. We have previously noted the process of disintegration in inanimate matter. Certain elements, if placed next to others, will unite with them. Sometimes this action is rapid—even violent. But there is no element of choice, no observable seeking, no demonstrated purpose.

There are, of course, mechanical factors in the fulfillment of purpose and in the attainment of freedom in all living things. There is the problem of the particular situation, and the efficiency of the mechanics of locomotion. Most plants and some animals are rooted to one spot and have no control over locale at all. They must seek such fulfillment as is available in the particular spots where their lots happen to be cast. Some animals build shells around themselves, thus increasing the purely mechanical nature of their lives. Even the development of skin covering, as in human beings, has significance in that it serves to protect us mechanically and reduce the freedom of intercourse with externality. On the psychological level, the barriers that we build may become so strong that freedom to seek and to receive may be almost eliminated.

Seeking the fulfillment of purpose and its implied freedom is, then, a powerful drive. It is a prime motivating force which goes back as far as life itself. It is a force to be reckoned with in any calculations as to what human beings will do under any given set of circumstances. The failure to recognize this fact may be the reason why economists so often turn out to be mistaken. They assume that the basic motive is economic and that people care most about food, clothing, and shelter. This assumption has been disputed by events throughout human history. Man will forswear his physical needs and comforts when his freedom is at stake. This is true at least of enough of the human species to account for the fact that tyranny, backed by the promise of material rewards, has always failed in the long run. (74)

The basic, organismic demand for freedom is, in one sense, limited and curtailed by the equally powerful need to be social. Man needs freedom and he also needs other people. But complete freedom may impinge upon and limit the freedom of other people. Therefore, these two needs have to be reconciled. No human being can exercise complete freedom to do as he pleases and retain his status with his fellows. He would soon be alone, deprived of one of the most important stuffs of growth, and in this solitary condition his development will be warped. This result can be observed in all people who are shut off from social intercourse with their own kind. (75)

In the discussion of cooperation we mentioned the naïve approach of those who think that beating others is the best way to get what they want. There is another naïve notion, held by many, that they ought to be free to do as they please regardless of others. Both of these ideas are naïve because they seem to be the simple, unsophisticated approach to fulfillment, whereas in practice they will fail to secure the satisfaction that is desired, because they thwart the social demand and drive people away.

The only real freedom that can be had is that which is possible within the social setting. When acts begin to limit and to deprive others, they become detrimental to the one who perpetrates them. The individual who sees that others are essential to him, that there can be no progress for him without others, sees the true significance of freedom. He then operates under controls which are self-generated, and his limitations are inherent in the social situation, rather than being forcibly imposed from without.

It might seem that this curtailment of freedom in its naïve sense is burdensome. The facts seem to be, however, that it is not stultifying, because of the satisfactions that come from the fruits of having others to provide what is needed for growth. It is better to be free to grow than to be free to do as one pleases. Old freedoms are relinquished for new and better ones. The list of freedoms that can be achieved by him who has become an effective member of a group would far exceed the number that could be listed for one who has isolated himself through the exercise of freedoms which drive people away. No new freedoms are acquired without the relinquishment of old ones. This is the new concept of freedom, called for in Chapter 1. It is a call for the relinquishment of the old, naïve concept of freedom, which amounts to license, and a call for the attainment of the possession of others. It is the relinquishment of limited personal gain for larger gains made through building others so that they in turn may build us. (76)

If these statements sound moralistic, it may be because morals have somehow often hit upon ways of living which are in keeping with the nature of living things. The teachers of the great religions, so commonly disregarded by those who profess to follow them, point ways which now seem to be scientifically tenable. Man's intuition has served him better than has his consciousness; for his conscious behavior has often contradicted his basic nature. This is said in the light of the prevalence of war, of personal conflict, of competition, and of license disguised as freedom. People seem to behave better when they rely on intuition than when they make conscious decisions, because their conscious behavior takes a limited, shortsighted, naïve view. But what is set forth here is derived from and can be supported by science rather than by any moral code. Such coincidence as there may be is probably significant.

If people are to acquire a tenable concept of freedom, the part to be played by education is great. Through education we have a chance to give to the young opportunities to operate in accordance with their own purposes in relation to a convenient social scene. The school has all the ingredients needed for practice in acquiring the larger, more liberating, and more tenable concept of freedom. Yet there are few places in our society where freedom is more curtailed, and where the significance of social intercourse is more denied, than in our schools. They are for the most part basically autocratic, and the unsocial are usually valued most.

The teacher tyrants are always defensive whenever anyone questions tyranny as a proper educative method. They usually say, "Do you want them to do just as they please?" They resort to ridicule, and invent stories in an attempt to make those who espouse the cause of freedom look ridiculous. They call upon all the inhuman devices known to man to reduce the questioner to a small and ineffective size. They do not want to face the application of the thinking process to their methods, but seek to keep discussion on an emotional level.

They know in their hearts that we do not want the children to do just as they please. We do want them to have an opportunity to work in accordance with their unique purposes, within the limits of their social milieu. We want them to be in bona fide social situations so that they may come under social controls. We want them to be put in situations where they will be forced to take responsibility for their own conduct. We want them to enjoy the benefits of larger and more lasting freedoms which result from social intercourse.

The tyrannical teacher, of course, behaves in a manner which seems logical to him. He is often controlled by his own ego demands. He attains size in a relative sense by reducing the size of others. He gains a satisfactory feeling of power by subjugating those who are weaker than he. Often he is unable to manage his world outside of school in such a way as to give him the satisfaction of power that his ego requires. One of the most tyrannical teachers we have ever known was badly henpecked at home. In addition, the tyrannical teacher ordinarily has had no experience with any other teaching method, and he can have confidence only in what he knows. He brings habit and cultural support for his method to the teaching task, together with a conscious or unconscious feeling of resentment for the freedom denied him in his own education, plus a desire to even things up now that he has at last come into a position of power over the weak.

The trappings of enslavement are well known. The typical classroom consists of rows of seats bolted to the floor. The moment the learner enters the room he can see that it is designed to restrict his freedom of movement, and that the room is so filled with immovable obstacles that social intercourse with fellow learners is certain to be greatly restricted if not impossible. It is as though learning was something that takes place during immobility, and that he faces being deanimated; he is to become a receptacle, and he must be held still for the filling.

Courses of study, textbooks, and lesson plans are designed, in part, to control and to delimit freedom. There may be times when the teacher, especially the young teacher, needs the support of a plan to use in an emergency. But the mature teacher who carefully plans all that is to go on in a given learning session has no intention of permitting the emergence of anything arising from the learners' purposes. To be sure, there should be a plan, but it must be made in consultation with those who are going to execute it. (77)

Obviously, the textbook is written and prepared in such form as to limit what is learned, rather than to extend it. To be considered a text, it must be thick so that it will last through the semester, and it must have questions at the end of each chapter so that the learner will not stray beyond its contents. It is said that teachers must have textbooks, since they are not well enough prepared to teach without them. This statement would not be true if teachers did not think they must determine what is to be learned before the learning can begin. Since the field of human knowledge is vast, if the teacher feels he must be the end-determiner, then he will need a neatly wrapped package which will serve as a crutch, because we are all lame when it comes to undertaking so great a task. The crutch rather than the healing has a way of becoming the end. Regardless of intent on the part of authors and publishers, the textbook is one of the important educational devices which result in limitation of freedom.

Probably the greatest robbery that it is possible to perpetrate on any human being is to rob him of freedom of thought, that which is often referred to as freedom of the mind. This is to rob one of what is distinctively human. Much of our education is designed to train people rather than to educate them. When one individual trains another, he delimits the variety of possible responses, making the desired responses automatic and eliminating the possibility of other responses. We can train lower animals, but we cannot educate them. Training, limiting possible responses, is enslaving, while educating is liberating. It is not that one is trained not to think, but that the act of training by its very nature delimits thinking. In the degree that the individual thus trained does think, he has been robbed of confidence in his own thinking. (78)

One of the outstanding characteristics of our classes in the training of inservice teachers is that they do not believe that any contribution they might make could possibly be worth anything. They are adults who are much schooled, and who, in comparison to the rest of the population, should be confident of their own ability. They have lost confidence in their own thinking.

It is here that indoctrination does its harm. Indoctrination is teaching in such a manner that the learner will not be free to change his ideas; so that it is impossible, or at least very difficult, for the learner to think differently from the indoctrinator.

Indoctrination is employed when we do not want to take the chance that the learner will disagree with us. It is used in the promotion of ideas, feelings, and attitudes in which the indoctrinator himself lacks confidence. For if the idea promoted is sound, one need have no fear that it will not be accepted by the learner if he is free to choose.

To be sure, no one escapes some indoctrination. One is most susceptible to it while very young, and we are indoctrinated, too, by our culture, if nothing else. This applies particularly to politics and religion, but it is effective in all other aspects of one's thinking and behavior. We can see this readily when we think of the difficulties we would encounter if suddenly we were deposited in a foreign land with a quite different culture. We would look and act queerly to the natives of that culture and be handicapped in social intercourse. As Sinnott says, "A Communist, a Roman Catholic, and a Protestant Fundamentalist would indeed be put to it to enjoy each other's company or profit from it." The answer to this, in the next millennium, is fluidity of peoples, which would tend to result in one culture. We do not, however, need to make matters worse by deliberately reducing freedom to think and to choose.

Propaganda is a device for indoctrinating people. The difference between propaganda and education is that propaganda is designed to establish beliefs and to exclude others, while education is designed to free the human mind. Propaganda is used to control thought, rather than to stimulate it. There is, therefore, no such thing as "good" propaganda. When a person speaks of being in favor of good propaganda, what he means is that he approves of one-sided and uncritical promotion of the ideas which he happens to believe. It is "good" to make people think as he does and "bad" to make them accept ideas with which he disagrees.

We often hear people say that we should indoctrinate for

democracy. This is an obvious contradiction in terms. Democracy demands complete freedom of the mind—freedom to think, to analyze, and to make decisions on the basis of this process. To be indoctrinated means to accept uncritically on authority, and if the acceptance is so strong that no other ideas can be entertained, all the better. The advocates of democracy who want to use indoctrination in order to promote it lack faith in it. If democracy is not the way of life that would be chosen by a free man, then there must be a better way of life. From what we know of the purposive nature of all life, and of the inherent demands for freedom, we have no need to fear that free men will not choose freedom. Those who wish to promote the democratic way of life would do better to see to it that people, particularly our youth, have opportunities to live freely so that they will have experience in, and know the values of, freedom. The way to learn how to live well is to live well; the way to assure ourselves that people will choose democracy with its inherent freedom is to give them chances to live democratically. We cannot expect people to choose the democratic way if we continue to indoctrinate them for autocracy.

To rob people of freedom of thought is to rob them of their most priceless possession and to take away their best chance for the life good to live. Many were the tragedies and crimes against humanity in World War II. Not the least of these was what was done to German youth under Hitler. Reports indicate that these youth had been so completely indoctrinated in the Nazi philosophy that to talk to them of democracy was futile. They had nothing with which to hear the words. They had been robbed of their capacity to entertain other than Nazi thoughts. Because they had lost their most priceless possession they were doomed, because the regime for which they had been prepared had vanished in flame. The creation of this condition in youth was possible because the indoctrination started at birth. Older Germans, who had grown up before the Nazi regime came into power, were more free to accept other ideas. Some of them, indeed, were able to become active advocates of freedom. (79)

We do not need to go to Germany in order to find youths and adults who are indoctrinated in authoritarianism. We see this in our students who want, and expect, us to make their decisions for them. We see it in adults who hold to the master-race idea or who believe in vigilante tactics. We see it in our superpatriots who want to crush all who disagree with them, and who, if successful, would destroy the very institutions that they seek to preserve. They violate the Constitution in the name of saving it. Hitler has given us a terrible demonstration of the power to destroy by robbing the individual of his freedom of thought. We would do well to heed this lesson while there is time.

This matter needs particular and thoughtful attention in these times because of the development of mass media for the dissemination of propaganda and its indoctrination. These media are the printed word in all its forms, radio, and television. The frontiersman did not live a very rich life, to be sure, but he was free from the constant battering we now take from all these sources. Since his mind was free, he invariably chose, and was willing to fight for, freedom. He did not go to school much, if at all, and was often illiterate, but he also escaped the authoritarian indoctrination of the school. In these times, because of the power in the hands of potential indoctrinators, our vigilance in preserving freedom of the mind must be constant and vigorous.

Closely related to the matter of freedom is that of discipline. We have seen that we operate under two basic demands in this regard. They are the demand for freedom implied by purpose and the demand for social relations with our own kind. The disciplined person is the one who attains his freedom through adequate social relations. The fact that others exist establishes restraints, through which larger freedoms are secured. The motivations are from within. The requirements of others may be thought of as coming from without, but the need to heed them is an inner motivation. The limits to unbridled freedom, which are inherent in respect for the rights of others, are the most wholesome sources of control. The need for rapport with one's fellows is the most powerful deterrent to unsocial conduct.

One cannot be mindful of the demands of the social situation if one is never cast in a social situation. The child or youth who is separated from his fellows by the trappings and methods of the classroom never has a chance to feel the need for rapport with his fellows. When thus isolated, and without this powerful deterrent, he is likely to behave in an antisocial manner. When his only deterrent is the authoritarian teacher, with whom he has never had or wanted rapport, his acts are likely to be directed against the teacher. The teacher then seeks to apply sanctions, and if they are severe enough they may serve to control conduct for a time, but they make the real situation worse instead of better. The child is so filled with unsocial attitudes that when he is out of reach of the autocrat and his sanctions he behaves less socially and adequately than he normally would. This behavior can be seen by standing outside the door of a repressive classroom as the class is dismissed. The children burst out of the room without regard for the fact that they may disable people who happen to be passing that way and who are not responsible for their state of being. In general, they are insensitive to others.

What the authoritarian teacher desires when he speaks of discipline is not discipline but obedience. He wants the purposes of others diverted and subjected to his purposes. This gives him a comfortable and orderly place to work, and gives him a feeling of power which gratifies his ego. But it is apparent that a purposing, freedom-loving individual must have a better reason for his behavior than the forcefully applied will of another. He can logically be obedient to his own need for fulfillment and to his need for others, but behavior other than this will obviously be illogical. All behavior, except that which is dictated and forced by another, is logical and is obedient to deep-seated natural requirements. These powerful inner forces which can produce the disciplined man cannot function unless teachers arrange settings where they can come into play. (80)

It is not likely that schools containing large numbers of uniquely purposive young can be operated without occasional resort to coercion. Coercion would be necessary in any event because children have not had enough experience to be as fully aware of the demands of the social scene as they will be later. This is especially true when children are conditioned to antisocial behavior in autocratic or anarchistic homes. It is akin to the situation in institutions for the mentally ill, where people go berserk and have to be physically controlled. But when we use coercion, we should do so with full knowledge of what it is. We should not be deceived as to what we actually accomplish. We should see coercion as a violation of basic principles seemingly made necessary because we have no other resource. We should be aware of the fact that the coercive act will do us more good than it will the child. Such an act is an expedient, employed until better methods present themselves. The objection to expedients is that they often seem to work so well, and to bring us so much gratification, that they become our accepted method of operation. The greatest danger in the use of coercion as an expedient is probably to the teacher rather than to the child. The one using coercion is in danger of becoming habituated to practices basically autocratic and unhuman. The child is damaged, also, but he will have a chance to recover when he escapes from the teacher, while the teacher will have to continue to live with himself.

Most of our schools, even today, have coercion as their basic method of operation. Many are the inventions teachers have created which are designed to defeat the purposes of the learners and bring them to accept the purposes of the teacher. If our teachers had spent as much energy and creativeness on inventing ways of improving the quality of living in their classrooms as they have in devising Machiavellian schemes for coercion, our schools would indeed be good places in which to live and learn.

Most of our coercive devices are applied to the mental rather than to the physical structure of our learners. They are what is described in our divorce courts as mental cruelty. But we are here forced to say that in many of our schools flogging is still in vogue. The medieval knout is still respectable in the middle of this century of enlightenment. We know a junior high school where it is reported not a single day goes by that the principal does not flog someone. In one school we know about, a teacher is designated as the whipping teacher. He deals out floggings on order, without knowing the recipient or the reason for them. The direction in which he must be growing and the end to which he will eventually come are matters sad to contemplate. We suppose that one must use physical force when one is completely outwitted and has no other resource. Logically, then, the more stupid and less resourceful a teacher or principal the more often he will have to flog. We know that in most schools flogging has been repudiated as an educative device, and that we have made much progress in this regard. But as long as there is any of it there is too much. We have to devote some space to this subject because the trappings of the concentration camp are still too prevalent among people who are entrusted with the task of stimulating the growth and development of our young. (81)

A low-level freedom is attainable under the autocratic teacher; in fact, one can have more freedom of a sort in the absence of rapport than with it. In the autocratic situation, one is entitled to do anything one can get away with. This is implicit in the situation. The autocratic teacher assumes responsibility for the behavior of the student, and therefore the student does not need to think about it. When one person assumes the responsibility for the behavior of many, there is certain to be a good deal of time when any one individual is not being watched, in spite of the fixed seats and the bird's-eye view enjoyed by the autocrat on the platform. If one is free to do as one pleases except when being watched, one can achieve a great deal of freedom, especially if one is courageous and resourceful. One will seek such freedom automatically because the situation demands it.

So it comes about that autocratic teachers are fair game. There is an open season on them the year around. This is the basic reason for the fact that, in our culture, youth and age are almost universally in conflict. This conflict is one of the saddest aspects of our society. We fight our youth, and they strike back, so that we actually live in two armed camps. We are thus deprived of the joy that can come from living cooperatively with our children. What should be our greatest fulfillment becomes our greatest burden. The adults, sad to relate, strike the first blow.

Because autocratic teachers are fair game, students cheat during examinations, use term papers they have not written, and resort to many other dishonest devices. These students usually regard themselves as ethical in all other respects. Cheating the teacher is in a category by itself and does not count when one's conscience calls for an accounting. This leads to a generalized attitude toward authority of all kinds, even toward the laws we all make together. This is the primary reason why an otherwise ethical person will cheat on our traffic laws. This attitude is partly responsible for the appalling slaughter on our highways. Irresponsibility, disregard of the rules, and bad attitudes toward all authority are the most common causes for this great loss.

There are many other evidences of rebellion against generalized authority in our society. The income tax cheats will serve as an example. People who consider themselves to be scrupulously honest in personal dealings do not hesitate to cheat the American people as a whole. They do not see the income tax in a social sense, but in an authoritarian one. They have Uncle Sam confused with the teacher or the parent, with whom rapport and its attendant obligation did not exist.

The student cannot cheat the teacher who is working with him rather than against him. He cannot cheat his fellows who are involved with him in mutual enterprises. His need for his fellows is so great that there is too much at stake to run such a risk. If he is to have freedom in the social situation, he has to achieve it through service to others and through improvement of his status with them. The person who is deeply involved in cooperative enterprises has much less freedom in the sense of license than he has if he is not so involved. He can, however, achieve freedom on a higher level. The chief cure for death on the highway and for income tax cheating is the building of social responsibility. This can best be done by practicing it in our schools.

The role of the teacher who is aware of the dynamic of growth is to provide freedom to grow rather than to restrict growth. The teacher needs to give free rein to curiosity so that the learner will be ever seeking new experiences. If the learner has this freedom he will, obviously, first become involved in current issues. It would not be sensible for him to start with those matters which are farthest away from him in time and space. Children would never by themselves start to study the history of man by going back to the ancient Greeks. They could start only with those around them. They would automatically settle the age-old educational question of scope and sequence. The sequence would be the order of things as he could reach them. The scope would be as far as he could reach. An educator never has to concern himself with the problem of scope and sequence except when he is deciding what another shall learn. Scope and sequence become problems only when the teacher has the limitation of freedom, rather than the extension of it, in mind. (82)

Similarly, the educator would be freed from the vexing problem of correlation and integration. The seeking learner who is free will never separate his learnings into the so-called "disciplines." As he goes about the business of investigating his environment he will naturally use and learn about all these "disciplines" together. They are not separate anywhere except in the classroom. They are separated because the teacher, as he plans what he is going to require the student to do, cannot imagine ways of tackling them together. Life comes to the learner correlated and integrated. If we do not take life apart, we will not have to put it together. As a matter of fact the separated fragments never do get put back together. (83)

As the learner seeks to know about current life he will inevitably encounter controversial issues. Current issues are most likely to be controversial because, being current, ready answers have not yet been found for them. Current and controversial issues are the growing edge of life and of learning. Issues which are not controversial have little or no significance except as they serve to throw light on controversial issues. Therefore, when we attempt to limit learning to noncontroversial issues, as we almost universally do limit it, we rob the learner of the part of learning that could make noncontroversial learning meaningful.

We can almost say that no learning which is not controversial is significant, because such learning deals with known answers only. We can say that known answers have significance only as they bear on answers yet to be found. Teachers who stick to noncontroversial learning think that they are playing it safe. They are robbing their charges, however, of freedom to live and learn. They are deliberately stultifying freedom in the interest of what they conceive to be their own safety. They are sucking the lifeblood out of learning. They are giving their students a pathetic demonstration of fear. (84)

Courage is the determination to assert freedom. It is the natural concomitant of purpose. It is essential to the maintenance of a free world. It does not have to be learned except by those who have been taught to be craven. Where it does need to be learned, it is best taught by example. Courage is contagious when one lives and works with people who are courageous. It comes with freedom, and preserves freedom. The teacher who reduces the courage of his learners robs them outrageously. The teacher who increases courage gives the learner the requirement for growing into a free man. (85)

If we are to have a free America or a free world, we must have people who have had their sense of freedom exercised. Freedom is worth fighting for; the world has been so constituted that the only freedom we have known has been secured by the violent assertion of it. We cannot expect freedom in a political sense unless we educate our people for freedom. We cannot stultify freedom in our young and expect them to develop into courageous, freedom-loving men. If we would be slaves, the surest way is to enslave our youth. If we would be free, our youth must have a chance to learn the meaning of the word.

CHAPTER 11

Creativity

And I know not if, save in this, such gift be allowed to man,
that out of three sounds he frame, not a fourth sound, but a star.

—Robert Browning

Life especially manifests itself in the creative grappling with situations which the world continuously puts upon us. This creative grappling considered in its continual effect on us is exactly education. Herein education is life itself.

—William Heard Kilpatrick

Whenever an individual takes a set of known answers and contrives a new response, concept, or artifact he is creative. It is the process of taking the things we now have or now know and putting these together in such a way that something new emerges. When we consider creativity we are inclined to think of the more difficult and abstract forms, such as painting, composing music, or writing great literature. Those are examples of creation on a complex level, and they have, of course, added greatly to our richness of living. So few people engage in these activities, however, that these complex arts constitute but a small part of the creativity of the human race. The great volume of creativity is to be found in the small and relatively simple operations of ordinary people whose minds have been kept free to contrive. Unique contriving is the flower of the thinking process. It can bloom only in a climate of freedom. It is the growing edge of discovery and invention, the method of progress.

The beginnings of contriving for new outcomes are buried far back in the history of living things. Long before the time of the first evidences of human existence which we can discover, man must have had some capacity for creativeness. He could not leave artifacts for us to find until he could make them. The development of written communication, even in the form of drawings, must have come late in his history. Even animals seem able to contrive for something new in a meager way. (86)

Contriving is probably a concomitant of life itself, since growth brings change, and change demands new answers. Creativity, then, comes on the very heels of growth. The development of new answers is part of, and inherent in, the dynamic of change. We can see that change, growth, and creativity are all one process and that they are inseparable.

So far we have considered creativity as an individual matter, and so it is in most cases. But a high level of creativity results when individuals contrive together. With any number of given, known answers, the imaginations, the contriving capacities of a number of people, when pooled, will produce more adequate new answers more quickly than can be achieved individually. Some of the most obvious possibilities are likely to escape the lone contriver. This idea is contrary to the commonly held notion that scientific progress, for example, has reached its high peak because research people have worked alone in competitive situations. If they had been pooling their ideas, there can be little doubt that they would have gone farther faster. The possibilities of group contriving are only beginning to dawn on us. Known answers are the foundation of all creativity. We must have something to contrive with before we can put things together in new ways for new answers. Probably the greatest value in known answers is that they can be used for new contriving. Indeed, this is the only value of a known answer. It cannot have significance except as it serves to enable the individual to live better, to live in new ways suited to his particular time in a changing world. (87)

While known answers serve as a foundation for creativity, they form an insecure base for continuous operation. Owing to the dynamic of change and to the uncertainty of knowledge, they will not abide. They are the best we know at any given time, and they are all we can have to operate with at that time, but some of them are not true at any time, and some of them lose their validity in changed times. If one could know all there is to know at the present time, one would soon be ignorant if one did not continue to acquire new knowledge. Order has a way of becoming chaotic, needing reordering. Certainties become uncertainties, verities become spurious, truth must be revised. This is the significance of change.

In this attitude we find the hardiness of the scientist. If he is to be any good as a scientist he must be able to accept new answers, and to let go known answers which no longer suffice. If his feeling of insecurity will not permit him to cut away from what he has held to be known, his laboratory will be of no use to him. He must be able to abandon what he has held to be true, and occasionally be willing to take what appears to be unprofitable risks for what seems to emerge as truth.

The problem-solving situation is the basis for creativity. As we go about our daily lives we are continuously cast in problem-solving situations. We see something we want to do, contrive a way to do it, try our imagined or projected method, and if it was well conceived, achieve our goal. This is a search for new answers and the relinquishment of old ones. It is a matter of wanting something new, of taking what we now have and of working it over to attain the emergence of something new. (88)

Problem solving is so essential to learning that it seems worth while to describe its elements. It consists of a series of steps, which in the doing are not recognized as separate.

1. The goal. The individual first conceives something he wants to accomplish. In this he sees something new, something he does not now have but which he thinks he has the means to secure or achieve. One of the most significant factors in this goal, an essential, is that he himself holds it to have value. He sees it to be worthy. All genuine creative contriving depends upon the goal being considered worth while by the contriver. Since life is not static, the goal does not turn out to be something to have and to hold, but it serves as a guidepost for more contriving. (89)

2. The plan. He then figures out a way, with what means or known answers are available to him, of achieving his goal. This is a process of projecting himself by his imagination into the position that he holds to be desirable. Unless he knows what he wants (the goal), and unless he can conceive a way of getting it (the plan), he will not be able to move from his present relationship and possession to the new one which he has conceived.

3. The attempt. Here he goes into action, using what he has in the way in which he imagined it could be used. Here he comes into contact with the concrete. Here he involves muscles, moves things or himself, reckons with externality, deals with its difficulties.

4. The evaluation. Plans do not always work. They cover new territory, and there is no way, except in trying them, to know whether or not they will succeed. The plan may be highly impractical from its inception. Unpredictable factors in externality may arise. Abstractions can leap over obstacles, but concrete action has to take them into account. When the plan is in process of being executed, and particularly if progress toward the goal seems small, the problem solver asks himself how he is doing. He asks himself— he does not wait for someone to ask him or for someone to render judgment. If progress is not satisfactory, he examines his calculations, tries to analyze his plan to see where it was weak, makes a more accurate estimate of the vicissitudes, and then revises his plan. He may need to make a new plan altogether because he may find from this evaluation that he is farther from his goal than when he started. Here the ability to abandon ideas is needed. Some people have great difficulty at this point because they are unable to abandon their previous ideas. They have a feeling of possession with regard to their original ideas, together with an unconscious feeling that they cannot be wrong. A feeling of ownership of an idea and the defense of it on that account can be a great handicap to creativity. (90)

5. The new attempt. Having revised the plan in the light of what may be an unhappy joust with the concrete, the problem solver tries again. There is no guarantee of success even now, for this is a new road. The process of evaluating, replanning, and trying again may have to be repeated any number of times. This depends upon the complexity of the problem, upon the skill of the contriver both in imagining and in dealing with the concrete, upon the scarcity of known answers with which to work, and finally upon the condition of externality—the difficultness of the terrain. Vicissitudes and temporary failures are to be expected. The only time that one must be right is the last time.

6. The achievement. If the contriver cares enough about his goal, and if it is not an impossible one, considering what he has to work with, he will continue to contrive, to try, and to revise until he achieves. Here, in this achievement, is something new, at least so far as he is concerned. Here is a new known answer which can be used as a guide for further contriving. (91)

This is the problem-solving process that is at the heart of creativity. So far we have considered it on an individual basis because that is simpler and more easily described. It is possible, however, for a group of people to agree upon a group goal which is held by each member as though it were his alone. The group can plan, try, evaluate, and achieve. This is a richer experience than that of an individual achievement because it contains the life-giving social element. It is a more cumbersome process because several personalities have to be taken into account instead of one. The achievement, however, is likely to be more satisfying because the imaginations, the powers of abstraction and contrivance of several people have gone into it.

In the previous chapter we discussed ways in which schools delimit freedom. In the degree that they curtail or deny freedom they curtail and deny creativity. The free person is creative; the enslaved one cannot be. We can observe this by watching a little child, who has not yet come under the influence of what we are pleased to call civilization, in action. All young children are creative. If there are limiting factors to their freedom in operation, they do not recognize them. All young children are curious; that is, they are searching for a knowledge and an understanding of their environment and are seeking new ways of using them to achieve new results. (92)

Curiosity is the urge to search and to contrive. It is the manifestation of a supply of energy seeking to spend itself. It is evidence of the existence of purposive drives. If we could retain the curiosity shown by little children throughout life, human achievement would be enormously greater than it is. We see, however, that as the child progresses through the grades of many of our schools he becomes less and less curious. By the time he reaches the secondary school he has almost ceased to be curious at all, at least about the program of the school. In many cases the drive to explore seems to have reversed itself so that he is not only uninterested in what the school has to offer, but is actually repelled by it. The curtailment of freedom, the demand to serve the purposes of others, has dulled the edge of growth and has deprived the learner of the use of the tool by which he can learn and grow. The teacher's problem then becomes most difficult, for he is forced to attempt the stimulation of a process which has been killed. (93)

One reason why teachers have such an effect on children is because we have grown too attached to known answers. Known answers are the foundation for any action or any creativity. But they are *only* the foundation. When we become too fond of them we lose sight of their purpose. Known answers are good only for contriving, but we accumulate them and then fail to go on to the action that can make them significant. It is another case, so common in education, in which the means becomes the end. (94)

The acquisition of known things has become a fetish. We have lost sight of freedom and creativity in the futility of a treadmill. We probably got onto the treadmill hoping to go places and to do things, but the growing edge of learning never came into sight and, through habit and inertia, we became fond of our imprisonment. We have even come to defend our chains and to claim that they are the desired goal of the creative, disciplined citizen. Like others who have been long imprisoned, we cannot imagine what we would do with freedom, and we cling to the security of our walls. We come to the point where we are ready to defend them as a desirable way of life. (95)

The degree to which we have become attached to known answers can be well illustrated by pointing out that a person can go from the first grade all the way through the graduate school without ever encountering a true problem-solving situation. In the assignment-recitation-examination routine, the goal is furnished by the teacher, and may or may not be shared by the learner. The teacher considers it immaterial whether or not the learner can see the goal as a worthy one. The plan also is furnished by the teacher, and he watches to see that there is no deviation from it. There is no need to evaluate because the plan has been tried many times before and is known to be correct. There is no freedom to make mistakes—the learner has to be right all the way. The achievement is automatic as long as the learner has followed directions. The answer is not a new one because the same road has been traveled many times by others, and it could have been secured from them. It is often to be found in the back of the book or in a pony.

This sterile process deprives the learner of any opportunity to assume responsibility for his own acts. His acts are confined to those which the teacher approves. Moreover, he is robbed of the freedom to make mistakes, which is essential to all contriving for there is much more to be learned by making mistakes than by doing things right. (96)

The student who is assigned a lesson and then studies it is not assuming responsibility. He is following orders—orders often backed by threats of punitive action. We often decry the fact that modern youth does not seem to be able to assume responsibility. The way to learn to be responsible is to have experience in it. If everything the learner does is planned for him, if all the juice of creativity is taken out of his education, if his experience is all in following orders, then he will not know how to assume responsibility. The way to learn how to be responsible is to have an opportunity to practice and to experience it. If the teacher takes all responsibility for the student's entire educational career, we cannot expect the learner to emerge a responsible person. He is certain to emerge a dependent person. This authoritarian method in which the goal and the plan are furnished by the teacher is the method followed by those who believe in training rather than in education.

Many teachers do not see the difference between an example and a problem. An example is an illustration of a problem which has already been solved. It is a repetition of a known answer. It has use in facilitating process because it can increase one's skill in the operation of certain segments of problem solving. It is no good until it is thus applied. The example is almost always used in the absence of any concrete situation to which it can be applied. It may be repeated endlessly without the learner ever being aware of the fact that it is something to use when desired ends are sought.

Teachers are often in despair when their pupils gain proficiency in the basic processes of arithmetic, but are completely lost when they encounter "story problems." They know how to add, to subtract, to multiply, and to divide, but they do not see that these processes have anything to do with the story problem. They know how to make these manipulations, but they do not know *when* or *why*. The story problems are themselves absurd when viewed from the standpoint of the child's world. Their answers certainly are not his goals. Even so, he might solve them if he had learned his operations in relation to any kind of problem situation instead of learning them in the abstract, much as he might learn a set of nonsense syllables. (97)

One of the great enemies of creativity is routine. Routine means that we do the same today as we did yesterday, last week, a year ago. Obviously, if we are going to do the same as we did before we will not create. In the operation of a school, particularly a large one, a certain amount of routine is doubtless necessary. Without it, the disorder would be too great for any accomplishment. The child needs to know, for example, where his place is in the school. He cannot have a feeling of belonging unless he has a place where he belongs. While a certain amount of routine is necessary, it constitutes a trap. Doing the same as we did yesterday is easy. Routinized children can be kept quiet, and an air of orderliness pervades the school. Teachers are more comfortable when the children are well routinized. We have come to think that a quiet, orderly school is a good school. We mistake the shadow for the substance. Quiet and order, rather than learning, become the objectives of the school. When beholding our neat package we forget that a person can be quiet and orderly without learning anything at all. We need to beware of the school that runs too smoothly.

Habits, which are built by repetition, are powerful. One is likely to be far more comfortable when he is following habit than when he is striking out toward new knowing. Many of our teachers have so habituated and so routinized their teaching lives that they are able to go through an entire semester without giving the whole matter a thought. The textbook is the great routinizer. This crutch enables teachers simply to give out assignments and to collect sterile answers. One reason why we have to have textbooks is that the lives of our teachers are so routinized and so sterile that they cannot imagine what they would do without them. Their creative genius, so evident when they were young children, has disappeared during a lifetime of disuse.

The routine nature of the lives that teachers live damages them even more than it does the students. While it is bad preparation for a life of contriving, after a time the students do escape from its stultifying atmosphere. The teacher, however, spends his whole career from first grade to retirement in it. This routinized life has a serious effect on the teacher, for all this time he is growing in a direction rather less than human. He spends his life enforcing routine, sitting on a powder keg of suppressed energy, avoiding the growing edge of learning and of life. He is seldom consulted about what is to go on in the school or even in his own classes. In this unproductive and uncreative atmosphere he grows less and less human so that, toward the end of his career, he is often sour and disagreeable, unable even to entertain a new idea.

Everyone is wondering when this teacher will retire, looking forward to that glad day, in face of the fact that, as the school is operated, more sour and disagreeable teachers are being grown to take his place. So it comes about that his retirement does no good at all because his place is filled by one much like him.

This situation makes no sense at all. If a teacher is growing in human, creative ways, his last years should be his best. Then, instead of his retirement being a cause for celebration, it would be a time of bereavement. Experience is the great teacher, but routine robs the teacher of it. If he has taught forty years he has not had forty years of experience, but one year's experience forty times.

The best time to avoid overroutinization, which is destructive of the creative life, is when the teacher is young. Older teachers can modify their methods in the direction of creativity, for we know that anyone can learn and change as long as he lives. But it is easier to avoid a trap than it is to extricate oneself from it. In most schools the young teacher will find an almost overwhelming demand to conform, to routinize, to get into the rut. If he can see the stultifying effect of such habit, he will resist it as he would arthritis or hardening of the arteries or any other limiting or crippling disease.

There are many ways by which the young teacher who is not already habituated can retain his zest for the new. Some of these will be discussed in the chapter on Method. He or she ought not to live alone if it can possibly be avoided. When one lives alone one has no one to whom to adjust at home. Rigidity of habit at home will be almost certain to develop, which will make it more difficult to be flexible at school.

The retention of flexibility—eager anticipation of change as against resistance to it—adds greatly to the richness of living. Most young teachers are idealistic—they want to do something in the service of mankind. They are not attracted to the profession for material reasons. They can best retain this idealism and accomplish this service by retaining their flexibility and their creativeness, for to retain these will keep them out on the growing edge of life, like the terminal bud rather than the embedded knot.

We are the products of the lives we have lived. If our older teachers are hard and unhuman, the school in which they have worked so long has made them that way. They were not hard and unhuman when they started life. If they are uncreative and afraid to venture a new way, they have been built that way by the lives they have led. They were not that way when they were four years old.

Here lies the most solemn charge to school administrators. It is incumbent upon them to see to it that the quality of living of the teachers in their schools is such that the teachers grow in human ways, that they feel encouraged to depart from the "tried and true." If the administrator can so organize his school that his teachers and students live together in high morale, and feel free to be creative and to depart from routine, the great human waste of the contriving genius of our teachers can be saved. One of the most profligate wastes of our society is permitting, even requiring, our teachers to function in ways which stultify their personalities.

Much change must come about if our schools are to become places where both learners and teachers enjoy the life good to live. Our schools have been solidifying in the opposite direction for a long time. This life good to live requires that the people live in freedom and creativity; that they have experience in contriving toward new ends. As they contrive toward new ends, other creative actions will evolve. To be alive is to be creative; creativity feeds on itself, as newly discovered answers become bases for more contriving. It is the method of growth.

CHAPTER 12

Evaluation

You can weigh John Brown's body well enough,
But how and in what balance weigh John Brown?

Stephen Vincent Benét

To evaluate is an integral part of life itself. It is inherent in everything we do. It is a process by which we judge what we perceive
and what we do in relation to our purposes and in relation to progress toward what we hold to be worth doing. Evaluation is a
continuous guide toward action or further action.

New concepts concerning evaluation are forced upon us by
recent discoveries in the nature of perception. These discoveries
show that life is almost completely subjective, for each one brings
unique experience and purpose to the perceptive process. Each
of us perceives a phenomenon differently from others because we
bring different experience and purpose to it. What we perceive is
uniquely our own, and the value of it is unique to each of us.
Evaluation, then, is unique, is subjective, and is continuous. (98)

There appear to be four factors involved in the perceptive process. There may be more, but at this time these four seem evident.
Two of these come before the perception; they make it possible.
They are experience and purpose, which have been previously
discussed. The other two seem to come after perception, but to
follow immediately and automatically. They are value and assumption.

As the organism makes its way through life it is primarily concerned with its own enhancement and defense. So, when anything
is perceived, it is instantly evaluated in respect to its possibilities to
the organism for weal or woe. "What does this mean to me? Is it

something which seems likely to enrich me, or will I need to fend against it?" This calls for a value judgment. A value judgment is a subjective evaluation of potentialities for good or evil to the organism doing the perceiving.

Feeling accompanies value judgments in most cases, but probably not in all. These feelings result from the evaluation. They range from extreme joy to extreme fear, depending upon whether that which is perceived is seen as greatly enhancing or greatly endangering. The emotional content of life depends upon the value judgments made with reference to the particular individual. (99)

We perceive many things in which we see little or no enhancement or danger. We are relatively indifferent to these perceptions, although we have the experience and purpose requisite to the perceiving. We doubtless make value judgments concerning them, but the value we attribute to them is little and the feeling is negligible. These perceptions lie in the middle zone between great enhancing value (great joy) and great endangering value (great fear).

Closely related to, perhaps even part of, value judgments are assumptions. These are based on unique experience and are unique to the perceiver. When we perceive anything we assume it is going to behave in a certain way or not behave at all, depending upon what we have observed in the past. We value in accordance with what we assume. If the assumed behavior is seen as beneficial, our values and feelings are of one sort; if the assumed behavior is seen as detrimental, our values and feelings are of another kind. The assumptions are, however, just as subjective and unique as any of the other elements in the perceptive process. No action would be possible without assumption and value judgment.

The evaluating that takes place in the perceptive process is on the unconscious level. It has been validated from the standpoint of survival and built into the very process of life itself. It probably had to be this way because if we had to decide consciously whether or not we would give value to a perception we might be destroyed while trying to decide. Many times in our long history we have had to fend quickly. The use of value has had as much need to be automatic as has heartbeat or glandular action.

Evaluation is an integral part of the problem-solving process, as we said in Chapter 11. It is automatic in the problem-solving process to a degree, as we are inclined to ask ourselves how we are doing whenever we try to reach a goal which we have accepted as worthy. It is possible, however, for us to go ahead without checking our success, and so evaluation of strivings toward a goal is not so automatic as that involved in the perceptive process. We may say that in separate perceptions evaluation is automatic and unconscious, but evaluation of clusters of perceptions, such as constitute a problem solution, while necessary for intelligent contriving, is conscious and not automatic. Evaluation, therefore, is something concerning which all intelligent beings need to give attention.

The solution of a problem produces a new answer, or at least one that is new to the contriver. New answers always require evaluating. Not all new answers are even tentatively true. It is through the evaluating process that the validity of new answers can be tested. Additions to human knowledge are made when new answers stand the test of validation.

All the evaluation that takes place in perception or in problem solving is subjective in nature. In perception, the question is, "What does this mean to me?" In problem solving, it is "How am I doing?" The questions have to do with the "I." The answers are made in terms of unique experience and purpose. They are personally made and held. They are part of the total experience; they are experience, and hence are built into structure. The organism is thus modified by these answers. Therefore, we may say that structure is being built. These answers affect the effective behavior of the organism, and from that time on they are part of it.

While each individual is the one who must evaluate his own progress, he needs also to be continuously cognizant of the social situation in which he operates, and the need to fulfill his social requirements. It is not enough for the individual to decide that he is doing well for himself. Others are affected by his behavior and are making their own subjective evaluations of the individual. Their approval is essential to him, because if he does not have it he will eventually be deprived of social intercourse. So the individual needs to ask himself not only how he is doing but how his behavior is affecting those around him. (100)

A great deal has been written and said about objective evaluation. This is the attempt on the part of one person to evaluate or to measure another person or thing. It occupies an important place in life, especially in the measurement of things. The objective measurement or evaluation, however, is always subjectively held and interpreted by the person doing the evaluating. We know that there is no such thing as an exact measurement, although materials are measured within an effective range. That is, they are measured accurately enough so that they can be operated in action. When people set out to measure other people, however, the measurements are so rough and the subjective element so strong that the measurement loses most, if not all, of its meaning. Experiments have been carried out where a number of teachers have read and graded the same examination paper, resulting in such wide disparity in grades that the results, one or all, could not be taken seriously.

This means that most of the so-called objective evaluation, especially when applied to other people rather than to materials, is found to be subjective, after all. If we are measuring a person we rationalize our results in terms of what we believed about that person before we started. When a "good" student does poorly, we say he was not feeling well that day. When a "poor" one does well, we say he was lucky.

There is no reason why we should not indulge in objective evaluation to the degree that we can do it. It is an error, however, to think such evaluation is something which it is not. If we know that our measures are inaccurate, particularly when applied to persons, we may be able, nevertheless, to get "straws in the wind" which will help us in making decisions. Immense harm can be done, however, if we are not aware of the limitations and so use our inaccurate and subjectively interpreted measurements wrongly in making decisions which affect the lives of others. At times decisions have to be made, but in making them many clues need to be accumulated and our own feelings need to be kept in check to the degree that it is possible. Then the decisions should be made with humility and with the realization that we may still be mistaken, rather than with arrogance and cocksureness.

Nearly all evaluation, whether it is called objective or not, is subjective in nature. If affects the evaluator more than the one being evaluated because it is an experience for the evaluator, and hence is built into his structure, causing him to behave differently to some degree in future action. The one being evaluated may assume a passive role, and thus not be importantly affected. One cannot assume a passive role when evaluating oneself. That is why subjective evaluation is an experience, while being evaluated by someone else may not be.

Better understanding of the nature of evaluation—its place in perception, in experience, in problem solving—will enable us to revise the evaluative methods now in use in our schools. School practice has departed a long way from meaningful evaluation, and the more we increase our effort in our present direction the farther away we seem to get. In schools, we have a way of drifting into practices which become habitual. It is easier to increase habitual activity than to be creative. The evaluative activities of the school have grown to enormous proportions. We need now to consider some of the errors or mistaken ideas into which we have fallen.

1. *We spend too much of our time in so-called evaluating.* Anyone can easily observe that, in our secondary schools and colleges, a significant part of the time available for learning is set aside for the examination schedule. Examinations usually take two or three weeks out of a semester, not to mention the time used by the student for "cramming," which scarcely qualifies as a real learning experience. This is in addition to the time taken for midsemester examinations and for the daily or weekly quiz. Formidable as this is, it is only a small part of the time spent on evaluative effort. The recitation, when the teacher asks the questions and the student answers them, is really evaluative in nature. If we were not such a serious lot we would see the incongruity of having the person who is supposed to know the answers asking the questions while the learner, who is supposed to be seeking answers, is expected to answer the questions.

So much time is spent in recitation, quiz, and examination that there is little left for learning. So it has come about that the institution designed for learning has become one which spends much of its time in testing what has been learned somewhere else. This is mostly done at home, in what has come to be known as homework. A shift has taken place so that we no longer send our children to school in order to learn but learning has been transferred to the home, and the role of the school has become one of measuring what has been learned at home and of issuing credits and credentials which certify that the learning has been done.

If learners spent six hours a day during one hundred eighty days a year in real learning situations where the evaluation was inherent in what was being learned, there would be no need for homework except for that which was self-imposed. There would be some of this because the learners would become so interested in the solution of what they were involved in that they could not resist such activity. Of course, parents have become fond of homework for their young because it tends to keep their children out of mischief and it enables the parents to shift their responsibility to the school. When the teacher assigns homework he is extending his authority over the child for the entire time, rather than just for schooltime. In our industrial society, where there is not much real work for children to do in the home, parents do have a problem in providing wholesome and useful activities for their children. But homework scarcely meets this need because only the conscientious children, who are unlikely to seek unwholesome companions and activities, do homework; the others simply reject it. Some of the conscientious and studious type work outrageous hours, and any teacher would rebel at the lack of leisure if it were imposed on him.

2. *Our evaluation is mostly objective.* Nearly all this enormous evaluative effort is objective, or extrinsic to the learner. It is an effort on the part of someone to measure and to judge the success of someone else. It is thus oriented away from self-examination, and of necessity becomes oriented to the subject matter. Obviously it must be oriented in some direction. We pay attention to what the boy does to the algebra problem, rather than to what the algebra problem does to the boy. It has to do with what the teacher thinks about the boy rather than with what the boy thinks about his own effort, efficiency, and effectiveness. What the teacher thinks about the boy is of passing moment, soon forgotten when he moves into another room. But what the boy thinks about himself is built into his structure and is permanent as long as he lives.

3. *We do not evaluate in terms of our purposes.* When anyone

tries to do anything he asks himself how he is doing in relationship to his purpose in trying it. This question is an essential element in all checking. Without it, checking has no meaning. Most people will concede that the over-all purpose of the school is to develop people who are adequate to meet life. While we spend the vast majority of our schooltime evaluating, we rarely evaluate in terms of our purpose. Rather, we evaluate in order to see how much of a specific area of subject matter has been remembered, although scarcely anyone would say that the remembering of this material is the purpose of the school. Whenever any experimentation is attempted in education, the experimenter is attacked because his work is said to be inadequately evaluated. The rejoinder could be that *no* school program is properly evaluated, if we take the larger purposes of the school as our guide. The experimenter might say to his critic, "It is true that we do not know much about how to test our effectiveness in terms of the adequate life to be lived by our learners, but neither do you. We have the advantage in that we do not spend most of our time evaluating something that is not directed toward our purpose."

Those who would engage in educational experimentation need to beware of a trap in this matter of purposes or of objectives. In many cases they have changed their objectives and procedures from those of the traditional program but have permitted themselves to be evaluated in terms of the program they have abandoned. All evaluation must be made in terms of purposes and objectives. When purposes, objectives, and methods are changed, outcomes will be different. Evaluation must be made in terms of what one is trying to do rather than of what someone else is trying to do. To illustrate: one teacher may spend a whole year drilling his students in grammar, while another operates a core program. The first teacher is apt to criticize the second because the students in the core program do not know grammar as well as do his students. The teacher who pretends that he can secure the same ends in a core program as another does by a year of drill is stepping into a trap. He presumably has abandoned grammar per se as a goal and has other goals which he believes to be more desirable. He must therefore insist that when judgments of success are made they be made in terms of what he purposed to do, not what some-one else aimed to do. (101)

4. *We accept symbols and give them meaning that they cannot possess.* In our schools at present symbols are attached to people. If a student is "given" an A or an E, he is in the way of becoming an A or an E person. The symbol comes to stand for human quality, and we are apt gradually to cease asking "A in what?" The whole business of human quality with all its nuances is forgotten in the thin air of abstraction. These symbols really can mean little in understanding flesh, blood, and attitude. Any of us who have at-tached these symbols to people should know this. They are cumu-lative in effect; it is easier to get the second A or E than the first one if the teacher giving the second one knows about the first. This is true in spite of the fact that the second teacher thinks he is strictly objective. He finds *his* judgment being tested as well as the performance of the learner. This process of abstraction is in its full bloom when the admissions officer in the college looks at the transcript and thinks he is looking at a person.

5. *We have been too fond of standardized tests.* When these tests began to appear on the market they were seized upon avidly. In the 1920's and 1930's we went through a spasm which has been referred to as the testing period in education. They were usually paid for by boards of education, were easy to administer, and helped to prove either that the teacher was a paragon or that the students were ineducable. Tests were an easy out for many of the evaluative problems of the teacher, for they helped to shift evalu-ative responsibility from the teacher.

The makers of these tests indulged in dubious practices. The tests were purported to test things which they could not test and were designed to measure things which did not exist. An example of this is the many intelligence tests. The intelligence quotient was the figment of the imagination of somebody; it was purported to be something an individual had in some degree and to be permanent and immutable, in much the same way that a person has a blood type. We now know that all IQ tests are related to culture and that one's intelligence in large degree is a product of the life one has led. We know that rich environments tend to produce intelligent people and starved environments are likely to produce dull people. We know that life is growth and that, when conditions for this growth are good, people grow and become more adequate to cope with life's problems. If this were not true, there would be little justification for the school as an institution.

Yet we have seen these IQ tests given to whole groups of students together, without regard for their condition at the particular time. Scores have been computed and have been used to categorize people from that time hence. In some schools these scores have been posted on the bulletin board. There have even been reports that teachers have seated their students according to the scores! Because of the weaknesses of the tests and because of their misuse and misinterpretation, we believe that as of today the testing movement has done more harm than good.

This does not mean that we believe all standardized tests are necessarily bad. We need to continue to work at devising instruments which will be valid—tests that will measure what we can hope to measure. The harm has come not from the nature of evaluation but from false claims for tests, commercialization of their sale, and from their misuse and misinterpretation after they have come into the hands of teachers.

It is not possible to make valid standardized tests except in areas where there are universally accepted goals. As we get learners to learning those things which are unique to them, and as learners have the opportunity to pursue unique purposes, we will have less and less need for blanket evaluation of any kind.

6. *We have not rethought the matter of standards.* When the secondary school was a small institution designed to prepare students for college and for the professions it was perhaps properly subject matter oriented. In the elementary schools of that time we tried to teach pupils to read, to write, and to cipher. We succeeded well with a few, but many did not learn much about the three R's and simply dropped out of school. A few went on in school but they were no problem in this area since they went on *because* they were no problem. We were thus able to hold high standards when judged in relation to the mastery of subject matter.

When we went in for mass education we were forced to modify

our objectives. Since only 15 per cent of our graduates, or about 7 or 8 per cent of those entering high school, are headed for college, it becomes absurd to operate the school as though everyone was going to college. We are forced to reconsider what the schools are for. We have to think about experiences that we can furnish youth that will add to the competence of those whose formal education ends with graduation from high school.

Because the school has changed its purposes have changed, and the standards to be applied also must change. This we have been reluctant to do. We have continued to try to hold subject-matter standards high, in the face of the fact that most of our students cannot, and will not, absorb the subject matter. We attempt to apply the standard of the small, select preparatory school to those who would not have gone to school in those days.

Instead of seeking new tenable standards, we have tried to make out by watering our subject matter down. We have not been happy about this. We still try to tell ourselves that we are true to our ideals, but we know that watering down is a surrender of principle. Our schools have many frustrated teachers who are trying most manfully to hold their outworn standards high, but who are being overwhelmed by great hordes who see little sense in their particular set of standards. Our teachers could gain great release overnight if they would rethink their function and accept the fact that what they once held dear no longer applies in this changing world. This they should be able to do without trauma, because there is nothing wrong with the standards they hold except that they are not applicable to the people with whom their lot has been cast.

We need to learn that few people—probably none in the teaching profession—hold low standards. Whatever standards any person holds seem logical to him, and arise out of the life he has led and the needs that press him. It is good for us to have high standards. They are the ideals toward which we strive. Accusing others of low standards is foul business because it implies depravity on the part of others and assumes unaccountable virtue for ourselves. Any teacher worth his salt has aspirations for his learners, but the aspirations need to be in terms of the learner's potentialities and purposes. For a teacher to permit himself to be frustrated because a boy who is mechanically inclined but linguistically inept does not glow over the quality of mercy being unstrained is a waste of pedagogical energy.

What we need is not a lowering or a weakening of standards, but a new set of standards to uphold. These new standards would not be oriented to subject matter at all, but rather to human growth. We would ask ourselves not "How much mathematics or history does he know?" but "How much has he grown as an experiencing, functioning individual? How well can he meet and adjust to other human beings? What will his attitudes be when he is confronted with decisions of war and peace?" In these areas we can establish satisfactory standards for ourselves with some hope of reasonably upholding them, and thus derive satisfaction instead of frustration out of them. We might call them human standards, and hold them high.

7. *We tend to be punitive about evaluation.* At first thought it would seem that there could be little relationship beween evaluation and punishment. As our practices have developed, however, punishment and evaluation have apparently become one and the same in large degree. We "give" good marks to people whom we want to reward and poor ones to people whom we want to punish. In class we suddenly call on the person who we think cannot answer or whom we suspect of "woolgathering"—another name for not attending to what we think is important. We do this because we want to embarrass and belittle him publicly. We invent trick questions for our examinations. If we can get a question which nobody can answer, so much the better, for then we can use our own discretion as to whom to punish because of it. We use threats of failure which we have the power to dispense or to withhold. This flaunting of power adds to our size and comforts our ego. We use the power which we hold through extrinsic evaluation to shift blame from us to others. If we have taught poorly, a good stiff examination will show that the ignorance and incompetence of our students were really to blame. We are thus able to emerge blameless from a situation about which we had had our doubts. Through rationalization we thus get someone else to bear the burden of our sins.

A good deal of our punitive action in evaluation is probably due to our insistence that our students do things for which they see no importance. If we are going to make people do things they would not do by choice, we have to resort to coercion. This coercion may be in mild form at first, but stronger medicine is called for as we go along. Resistance on the part of the learner—and he is bound to resist—becomes personal. It is transferred from the task the learner does not want to do and becomes a personal affront to the teacher. Then the egoistic drives of both learner and teacher are involved, and there ensues a dirty fight which has little relation to what started it. What started out to be a lazy form of motivation often ends in a blood feud. All the decent objectives of school—adequacy, learning, growth—are completely forgotten.

8. *Evaluation tends to become an end rather than a means.* This is a common institutional danger. We can observe it in innumerable places in the school. Mathematics is now mainly taught for itself and not as a means for solving human problems. Grammar, the explanation of language usage, has become a good in itself. School offices established to facilitate learning now operate as though the school was maintained for the offices. Students' programs are often left unchanged because of what a change would do to the office. Financial transactions can be made only if they fit the accountants' books.

In no area is this more true than in evaluation. The moment an evaluative procedure is established, that which is taught is changed to meet it. A standardized examination immediately becomes an end-determiner. What started to be a measure of what is learned becomes what is taught. Many a tail wags many a dog. This can perhaps best be illustrated by observing what goes on in the high schools of the State of New York in connection with the Regents' examinations. The examinations in considerable degree establish the curriculum. The teachers of the state are more responsible for this than the Regents are. The teachers could get rid of these examinations if they really wanted to.

If an evaluative instrument or device has any value, that value is obviously diminished or lost when teachers begin to teach for it. Modifying what is taught in order to pass a previously established examination is not desirable, but stultifying, when general education is the objective and general competence of the learner is the goal. Whatever we do in evaluation, we need to be careful that the evaluative instrument does not become an end-determiner, because if it does it will lose its usefulness as evaluation.

The greatest undeveloped frontier in education today is evaluation. There is no other field about which so much has been done and concerning which so little is known. This is because our efforts have been spent in extrinsic evaluation—somebody measuring somebody else—when it comes about that the only evaluation that really has much to do with growth and with the building of structure is intrinsic and subjective. We have literally mountains of tests, nearly all extrinsic. We would be appalled if we could see all of them in one heap.

It is true that a few of our tests are intended to bring about self-evaluation. Also, some of our examinations are designed with that end in mind, but this is not true of most of them. We need to invent new ways of securing self-evaluation. There may be instruments not yet designed which will serve this purpose.

We can teach problem solving if we put our minds to it. There are logical steps which can be taught and can be followed. There is logical order in going about the business of doing what one wants to do. It can best be taught by putting people into problem-solving situations which constitute real problems, not examples. For that matter, it is hard to see how we have become so involved in evaluation, because it is simply a matter of asking ourselves how we are doing. Asking ourselves does not mean asking somebody else or having some other person tell us. (102)

We can invent more and better ways of throwing the responsibility for learning on the learner instead of carrying it ourselves. When the learner is responsible he has to ask himself, from time to time, how he is doing.

We can come to grips with the marking system and, instead of complaining about it, can work out some sensible action to take its place. The marking system has been under fire from many sides for a long time. It has been about thirty years since most schools abandoned percentage grades and substituted letter grades. This change was a recognition of the fallibility of the percentage grades. This was a minor reform, but it showed the beginning of dissatisfaction with our early methods. We can isolate the purposes of the grades and can substitute better methods for them after we see what they are for. If the purpose is to report to parents, better ways for doing that can surely be devised. If it is to send to college or to an employer, we can invent better ways of telling these officials what they want to know. If grades are for the purpose of making people work, let us admit that fact and let us see if we cannot find more wholesome reasons for human activity.

One objective measure that might do us all good is to decide what the school is for, and then, through follow-up studies, to see how our products are living. Examination of the success or failure of our students as adequate, competent citizens is probably the best measure of the success of a school. We must, however, be careful to do it well so that our failures as well as our successes will be identified, and we must have some agreement as to what constitutes success.

The problems of revamping our practices and our attitudes in the area of evaluation are enormous. They call for a whole new approach to learning and to teaching. At present we know so little about evaluation that we scarcely know where to begin. That is why we say that it is education's great untouched frontier.

CHAPTER 13

Method

Our task as educators is to begin with life, to nurse it, to help it to grow, to help it enrich itself, always so that more of life may result in the person himself and in all whom he touches. There is no richness but life itself.

—William Heard Kilpatrick

Considering what we now know about the nature of the human organism—how it perceives, learns, and grows—great changes will have to come in the area of teaching method. Perhaps it is in this area that educators and teachers show the sharpest disagreement. To be sure, we have much disagreement on what to teach, but when we concede that all knowledge has some value to somebody we admit that the value of the learning is a matter of degree. We can contend that while the learner is learning one thing he might have put his time to better use if he had learned something else. It will not pay us to contend that a specific item of knowledge is bad in itself, but we need to raise the question as to whom it is good for, when, and why.

There is also the question as to what it is possible for a specific learner to learn. The learner has to have some experiential background for what he is to undertake to learn and some purpose which seems reasonable to him. When our methods do not take these matters into account, the learning we intended to teach will be slight, although other things which we do not intend to teach are likely to be learned.

The importance of method can be seen when we realize that the method used controls what is taught. What the teacher does largely determines the kind of people he will develop. The authoritarian teacher will develop one kind of person, the democratic teacher another. Human growth takes place in one direction when the learner is having things done *to* him and in another when things are being done *with* him. He tends to grow in human ways under a human method, and in inhuman ways under an inhuman method.

The curriculum itself is modified when method is modified. Indeed, revising method is the easiest and most sensible road to curriculum revision. When teachers change from authoritarian to democratic methods, what is learned will change also. As long as teachers are deciding by themselves what will be taught in an authoritarian way they are simply trading one item for another. This type of change can result in some improvement, but it is still guesswork so far as what ought to, and can, be learned by any particular learner. When the teacher begins to derive his curriculum from the learners he will discover that not much of what has previously constituted the curriculum will be included. (103)

Democratic teaching involves just as much change in what is taught as it does in how it is learned. Modification of what is taught is an essential in any democratic method. Too often we do not see that there are two sides to a change from autocratic to democratic method. Teachers who become "converted" to democracy as a teaching method and think that they are going back to their schools to teach the same things they have been teaching, except that they are going to do it democratically, are sure to fail. There are some things which simply cannot be done democratically. It is not possible, for example, to give a horse a dose of medicine democratically. If the teacher retains values which he cannot abandon and which his students cannot accept, he will not be able to behave democratically. Teachers who want to be democratic but cannot surrender the idea that they have values which necessarily have to be substituted for the values of others and who hold in low esteem the values held by others will need to review their democratic philosophy. (104)

We have suffered from confusion concerning the difference between people and things. We have had many "how" books which have dealt with how to do things to people whom the authors of the books have never seen. It is possible to give the "how" when the objects concerned are inanimate, but not so easy when unique human beings are involved. We can tell on paper how to plant a shrub or how to build a radio, but shrubs and wires do not have unique personalities to take into account. Teachers are often hoping that someone will tell them how to deal with Johnnie next Monday, although the person giving the advice has never seen Johnnie. Such devices are called "tricks of the trade" and come to be recognized by students as tricks. They are ways of doing things to people rather than with them. People who want to know how to do things to other people—to make others over to suit their ideas —are liable to indulge in dangerous meddling with the lives of others, and are likely to get results contrary to those they expected. This meddling assumes a superiority on the part of the teacher, a teacher-knows-best attitude, which is hard to justify.

If we are to see the end of "how" books as applied to human affairs, we may also hope for an end to courses in methods which are aimed at the same devices. In the training of teachers we now have many methods courses which are designed to transmit, verbally and by means of reading, the tricks of the trade. Not infrequently the methods used in the methods courses belie what the teacher-trainer says about method. The teacher-in-training learns far more from the method used than he does from what is recommended. Every course, particularly in teacher training, is an eloquent methods course because it demonstrates a method, and teachers naturally learn to teach by the way they have been taught. If a teacher wants to teach democratic method, he can best do so by teaching democratically. If he demonstrates good method, he will not need to set up special courses to talk about method.

Since learning is growth and has to be done by the learner in the light of all his uniqueness, the area of teaching method becomes one of doing things to the circumstances under which the learner tries to learn, rather than of doing things to the individual. If we may recall the illustration of the gardener and the tomato plant, we will realize that many things can be done in order to arrange circumstances under which growth will be propitious. We cannot do the growing. Method involves arrangements and conditions, not the forceful making over of people in our own previously held images. (105)

The conflict in method among teachers hinges on what the

teacher believes about the proper source from which items to be learned can be drawn. These beliefs extend beyond teaching and learning to basic ideas about other people. The authoritarian teacher believes that he is best able to decide what shall be learned and that, if he does not decide and enforce, nothing will be learned. He thinks that children not only are lazy, but perverse as well, and he sees himself as a correctionist. These beliefs call for a method. First the learner must be held still, for he is going to have something done to him, somewhat in the manner that a calf is tied for branding. Communication between learners must be reduced, and, if possible, eliminated, because the communication is to come from the teacher; it cannot come from the learners, for they do not know what has been decided upon to be learned, nor would they have any significant contribution to make if they did know.

The device for securing the deanimation of active youth is the arrangement in rows of seats screwed to the floor so that the only view the learner gets of other learners is the back of the neck of the one seated in front of him. Often, children are required to fold their hands on the desks and to stare ahead so that involvement of their muscles will be reduced to a minimum. When the animate in the learner has been reduced to the inanimate, the teacher is ready to pour out the learning.

When the results obtained by this method are disappointing, the teacher steps up his punitive methods. He increases the punishments, he grades the students more sharply. The patrons of the school see no way to better results other than to demand that the teachers "crack down." The teacher's answer to his failure is to do even harder what he has been doing wrong. This method results not in more learning but in more rejection of the curriculum by the learners. The learners withdraw from the uneven conflict, as anyone of sound judgment would do. They withdraw not only mentally but physically as well, as can be seen in the shocking figures on "drop-outs" in our secondary schools.

So far as we know there is not one shred of scientific evidence to support the deanimation and crack-down theory of learning. Yet those who use it contend, curiously, that they are scientific. Great strides have been made in recent years in the understanding of the nature of the human organism, but none of the research known to us supports this theory. When asked what scientific support they rely on for their method, the supporters of the crack-down theory say that it is obvious that this is the way to teach because teaching has always been done this way. Some of them say that they have tried democratic methods but that such methods will not work because the learners are perverse. Others point to the fine young people who have come through their classes, have gone to college, and perhaps have even become teachers like themselves. The witch doctors supported themselves for aeons, and still do, by pointing to those who survived their medicine rather than to those who did not.

The crack-down method is sometimes supported by pointing to the alleged success of the method in the armed forces. Not much is known about the actual success there, but the analogy breaks down at its inception, for in the army the conditions are different, and the motivation is different. When what is taught may have the survival of the learner at its base, we are apt to have willing learners. Anyway, our students are not in the army, even though some of us wish they were. (106)

If there is any scientific support based on the nature of the organism which indicates support for the crack-down theory, it should be brought forth. If science indicates that the method is contrary to fact, the method ought to be abandoned.

The democratic teacher believes those things which are consistent with the ideals of democracy. Some of these are that every human being has purposes, needs, wants, and that what is learned can best be derived from these. Communication is at the base of learning, and the more of it that can be secured in the classroom the better. Two-way communication is better than one-way because every person involved has unique experience and therefore has a unique contribution to make to others. Insignificant as the learning derived from the learner may seem to the teacher, it is at this precise spot, and only at this spot, that real learning can begin. The democratic teacher believes that people are not lazy or perverse when serving their own purposes; that nobody wants to serve the purposes of others; and that learners are as virtuous as teachers in this regard. He believes that the best way to teach democracy is by example. (107)

The pressing problem confronting the democratic teacher is to devise a method which will square with the democratic ideal and one which will work. To devise such a method would be natural and easy if the culture from which his learners are drawn were democratic. The climate of most American homes is either authoritarian or anarchistic. The young are therefore conditioned against the assumption of responsibility which is implied in democratic function. This adverse conditioning has to be overcome, and it can be overcome, as is shown by the work of a good many democratic teachers.

It is at the initial state that many teachers of good will fail. They attempt too much too soon, without taking the adverse conditioning of their learners into account.

Let us see what principles of method may be useful to the democratic teacher. Method is a matter of principle rather than a specific. It has to be geared to particular situations, the specifics of which can never be anticipated. This is the difference between the trick of the trade and sound foundation in method. If we can have principles toward which to work, the details of the specific situation can be uniquely worked out in the light of them. Tricks without principles will hardly serve to steer an intelligent course.

The first principle to take into account is that we learn best by the involvement of the total organism. Therefore, we should construct a method which will involve as much doing as possible.

We have heard so much for so long about learning by doing that the words seem trite. John Dewey has been telling us this principle for at least sixty years; probably there is not a teacher or administrator anywhere who has not heard of it. The vast majority accept it as truth. Little has been done about it. We will have to continue to hear about this principle until we seriously take it into account in our method.

In recent years research has added to the validity of this concept. It has seemed obvious for ages, because anyone who is being given instructions as to how to do something always asks to try to do it. His awkward movements become skilled as he does it, not as he listens. We would hardly expect a man to be able by verbal instructions to learn to tie a bow tie on himself. We now see that the human organism is a totality and that we do not have a mind removed from a body to train. The organism learns as a whole, as a totality. Muscles learn as an integral part of the whole. So in any learning—if we can involve the total organism, we can accomplish complete learning. Every portion of the totality has to adapt to a specific purpose. When the total organism is involved, as it is when it does something, the fulfillment of purpose has a residue which is manifest in the whole. The organism is different as a result of it—behaves differently—and this modified behavior is the evidence of learning. Confidence is born of total involvement in successful fulfillment of purpose. When one knows he has accomplished one thing he has the courage to attempt another, which may be more demanding. All of this was not so easy to see as long as we clung to the mind-body duality.

One reason why learning by doing has not made more progress is that it calls for modification of what is to be learned. It is difficult for large numbers of students to learn about the binomial theorem or the ablative absolute through total involvement of the organism. Changes in method call for changes in curriculum. We will have to begin to think of things that people can do. Some of our sacred cows will have to be sacrificed. Of course one of the reasons why so little progress has been made in this regard is because education has been so miserably supported. No one can do unless there is room to do and things to do with. It is cheaper to put a learner in a few square feet of space at a desk and put a book in his hands, which in many cases he has bought himself, than it is to give him a hammer, a saw, and boards, and the room he needs in order to operate them.

A teacher seeking an improved method will look to see what arrangements can be made to increase the doing that is available to the learner. This increase in doing may be little or great, but whatever it is it will be a move in the right direction. The modification of what is learned will doubtless also be in the direction of a more functional curriculum.

At best, a great deal of what goes on in our classrooms as now constituted must be on a verbal level. Verbal participation is a form of doing, better than none, although it does not involve as much of the total organism as doing which calls for more physical activity. When a learner participates verbally he can gain great satisfaction from the feeling that he has been a part of what has gone on and that, whatever comes of it, he helped to make it.

Much can be done as method to make physical circumstances such that the organism is open to receive and ready to contribute. The most obvious change is to rearrange the seats so that the people who are going to participate can see each others' faces. We cannot communicate with others as long as we are gazing at the backs of their necks. When learners are seated so that they are in a position to exchange ideas, the teacher can do some things which will tend to relax the learners, so that ideas may have a chance to penetrate the learners. In this setting the teacher will not need to demand attention, because not all that is to be learned will be coming from the teacher. The word "attention" means at-tension. People who are at tension are not in the best condition to communicate. The learner who sits with notebook and pencil poised is apt to be more concerned about his notes than about his learning. He is not prepared to give anything. He has a bad effect on the teacher because the teacher may feel impelled to try to say something that is worth taking down.

The relaxed and comfortable person is in the best state to give and to receive. He is not necessarily inattentive, any more than the rigid, poised, uncomfortable person is necessarily attentive. When the learner is relaxed he is more open to ideas. His psychological barriers are reduced. The tempo is likely to be one which he feels he can keep up with should he want to contribute.

Merely changing the physical arrangements will not produce a good learning situation. We have seen teachers go to a good deal of trouble to get students into a circle where each can see all the others and then behave exactly as he would have behaved had there been no change. The most important relaxation is psychological, and this comes from the permissive attitude of the teacher, although it is promoted and made easier by propitious physical arrangements.

There are of course a number of physical details besides seating which will occur to teachers who believe that learners accomplish more when they are comfortable. It seems hardly necessary to detail here the fact that human beings need light, but not in their eyes; that they need fresh air and comfortable temperature. They do best in situations which are reasonably attractive with color that is conducive to comfort. It seems incredible that schools and schoolrooms could be so drab and uninviting as they often are. All these items are part of method because they have to do with the arrangements through which growth may take place.

Breaking the class down into small groups is a method or arrangement which has great promise for involvement, participation, and communication. This is especially true when it is possible to get people together who are interested in the solution of a particular problem. Such a grouping can usually be accomplished if it is worked at. There is not space here to discuss the small group technique fully. It has been written about in considerable detail in other places. If we believe that communication is essential to learning, we will have four people at a time instead of one, communicating by breaking a class into four groups. If we believe that people need to be interested in what they are learning, a learner has four choices instead of one. (108)

The small group technique is of great promise and great usefulness. It is not good-in-itself, but a tool to be used when it will do what is held to be desirable. Like any other method, it needs to be used when it will serve a purpose better than some other method. We have seen teachers who seemed to think that all they had to do was to place their students in small groups, and that growth would be automatic. In using any method we have to assure ourselves that it will do what is expected of it.

The democratic teacher will inevitably incorporate teacher-learner planning into his method. It is unthinkable, when one stops to reflect on it, that a group can enter into an enterprise when only one in the group knows what is to be done and has made the decision all by himself. Whenever a group of people start to do anything, consultation is required if the project is to be anything but authoritarian. Consultation among those who are going to do a project is not only a matter of ordinary decency, but also it has many advantages in itself.(109)

One who has been consulted about what he is going to do approaches the task with a quite different attitude than one who has not been consulted. Attitudes release or withhold energy for a task. The consulted person feels that he is a factor in what is going on. He has a feeling of involvement which cannot be secured by coercion. Without consultation, he feels that this is the teacher's show, and he has no responsibility for its success or failure. When the teacher does all the planning, he also assumes all the responsibility. As a result he is liable to get apathy on the part of the learner at best, if not active resistance.

The teacher who enters into planning with his learners, however, must be ready to accept what is planned. He must be ready to abandon his own goods for the goods of the group. If he has his mind made up in advance as to what is going to eventuate from the planning, he would be better off to go ahead with his own plan without any pretense of consultation. We have known teachers who entered into planning with their learners but vetoed every suggestion until the one that they had in mind in the beginning came along. This behavior is insincere and dishonest. The learners see through it, and it lowers their estimate of the integrity of the teacher and makes rapport more difficult to establish.

Teacher-learner planning, then, is a requirement as method in democratic teaching. The great handicap to its extension as method is that too few teachers are willing to surrender their preconceived notions as to what is going to be done. (110)

A technique closely related to teacher-learner planning is that of student participation in school government. The government of the school affects everyone in it. The governmental arrangements or rules have to be made either with or without the consent of the governed. In most of our schools the rules are made without the consent of the governed.

Citizens in a democracy have great need for experience in the practice of citizenship. The school provides an ideal place for such experience because it has most of the problems of any society, except that they are usually less acute. The development of democratic citizens is perhaps the primary charge upon our schools. The schools themselves cannot long survive without competent citizens to support them. (111)

For the most part, we have tried to produce citizens and to build character by telling people what is right. We have not succeeded too well. We should have learned by now that people do not behave badly because they have not been told the difference between right and wrong. Character is not something people possess apart from the product of total experience. Preachments often impel people to do the opposite. Add coercion to preachment and we are almost sure to build up motives in opposition to what we have preached. This opposition is especially likely to develop among people who take their counsel from courage rather than from fear.

Student participation in school government can produce citizens who have had experience in governing themselves. It is a device for involving the students in the program of the school. It can make each member feel that this is *his* school, not the teacher's. Character is built when people are involved in the life good to live.

The same confidence in others and the willingness to abandon preconceived ideas are as much required for the operation of a system of student participation in government as for teacher-learner planning. If we do not have faith in the rightness and goodness of others, we will not be able to enter into sincere student participation either in government or in planning. The chief reason why student participation in government has made so little progress is that administrators and teachers have been unwilling to surrender their own previously held prerogatives. They simply do not believe that young people can, or will, assume responsibility or make sound decisions. This attitude has caused the development of many so-called student councils that are really shams, because the councils do not make any important decisions nor affect the lives of the students in any way.

Student participation in school government is a method or technique for securing involvement through consultation. It is a method holding great promise for those who have the faith and courage to use it.

Teachers who teach under adverse circumstances often ask what they can do to take into account modern knowledge of the nature of the human organism and its ways of learning and of growth. The methods so far described and implied require a reasonable adequacy of physical setting. They require that the room in which learning is to take place be larger than most of our classrooms, for learners need room to move around, to rearrange their chairs, and on occasion to form small groups. The room needs to have decent light, heat, and ventilation. It should be richly stocked with materials which can be used by the learners without leaving the room. It needs to contain few enough learners so that the group will be manageable as a learning and working group. No one knows what the maximum class size should be, because the size should vary with what is going to be done, with the adequacy of the facilities, and with the skill and temperament of the teacher. It is probably safe to say that no class should have over twenty-five members unless it is going to spend its time looking or listening.

Most of our teachers do not teach under such conditions. Boards of education engage in false economy by giving teachers more students than they can teach, and by failing to provide adequate room for them. Citizens know that it is not economical to give a factory worker twice as much work as he can handle at his station. But they seem to feel that there is economy in giving teachers twice as many students as they can teach. When they put forty to fifty students in a room that can accommodate twenty-five comfortably, they actually lose their investment by creating a situation where real learning cannot go on.

It is presumptuous of us to think that we can expect much modification of method when teachers work under such circumstances that they cannot hope to give much more than custodial care to their children. They become mass baby sitters at a ridiculously low fee per child per hour. Sometimes we wonder if custodial care is not what parents are really most interested in, considering the facilities and numbers they provide. (112)

There are, however, some items in the area of method which any teacher can use, no matter how difficult the conditions under which he is obliged to work. We need to consider what we can do in the direction of being human and of evoking human responses from our students.

No matter what our circumstances may be, we can meet our classes with a friendly attitude. Too many teachers go to class expecting a fight. The best way to get a fight is to expect one. We can let trouble come to us, as it probably will in some degree, without looking for it. This friendly attitude will reduce the need for punitive action. We will see less and less need for doing punitive things to people. The requirement of a friendly attitude is not soft stuff. Nothing is more powerful in the development of human relations than the attitudes with which people are approached. Whatever the attitude of the teacher may be, it evokes similar ones from the students.

We can extend friendship on a more personal basis to the students who need it most. We probably cannot have personal friendly relationships with all our students, but in a group of forty it is not too difficult to tell who are the most friendless and therefore need us most. Friendliness may mean a great deal to certain children. Some of them are much alone. The teacher is often the one person most able to extend this friendship. Howard Lane, who has had much experience with delinquents, has said that no child who has one genuine adult friend becomes delinquent. This statement may be too sweeping, but there is doubtless great truth in it.

We can retain our sense of humor. This will keep us from being too easily affronted. When we lose our sense of humor we are apt to take as personal attacks things which ought to amuse us. In a room overfull of restless and energetic youngsters, events are likely to occur which are simply the result of too much energy confined in too little space. The teacher who thinks outbursts of this energy are especially designed to bedevil him is liable to suffer from a battered ego before a day is ended. What was not intended as a personal attack can become personal in intent if it is accepted that way by the teacher.

We can control our language. This applies to what is said and how it is said. We extend ourselves unduly when we think we have to shout at people, sometimes with voices so raucous that they should never be let out. The well-modulated voice secures more attention than the shout.

What is said, and the manner and tone of it, either increases or decreases distance between teacher and learner. The control of pronouns will have much to do with the problem of distance. "You" tends to put distance between people, while "we" tends to draw them together. "I" excludes the other, and, since he is excluded, he fails to partake. Our prepositions also need watching. There is a great difference between doing things *to* or *with* another. A common student expression indicative of faulty teaching habit or method is shown when a student says, "I had a course *under* Professor———." In many cases, we fear, the learner is really *under*, not *with*. (113)

Language, as well as materials, needs to be suited to the maturity and readiness of the learners. That is, our language must not be over their heads nor seem to imply that we are talking down to the learners. We often affront young children by talking down to them, almost sinking to the use of baby talk. Children like to be treated as people, as peers, and one does not talk down to peers. The vocabulary has to be suited to them in their stage of development, but need not be condescending.

No teacher need ever resort to sarcasm or ridicule. They are devices intended to reduce the size and importance of others; to "cut them down to size." These devices are basically degrading in intent. When the teacher wants to cut anyone down to size, he is inadvertently admitting his own small size and is seeking to grow big by the reduction of the size of people around him. If everyone else is small enough, and is "put in his place," the teacher can feel quite big. Cutting others down is quicker and requires less time and effort than are required to grow big.

These latter suggestions in the area of method are minor, but they are ones that can be used by any teacher no matter how difficult his situation. They are not real solutions, for real solutions depend upon improved conditions for teaching and learning. They can be useful, however, to discouraged teachers who, because of the crowded conditions of their classrooms, can see little chance for real human relations in their classes. These suggestions are in the direction of humanizing what will be at best a sorry substitute for a real learning situation. They will enable such teachers to come away from a day's school with a cleaner feeling than is possible when the day has been spent in combat.

Teaching is a human business, and the methods employed in it must be those which add to the human qualities of the learner. When people of integrity operate, method springs from principle —from beliefs held. Human beings need each other, and methods which bring them together serve them well. Individuals are unique, with unique contributions to make, and circumstances need to be arranged so that these contributions can and will be made. We want to have done with the invention of ways of doing things to people and to concentrate whatever inventive capacity we have to the improvement of circumstances which will be propitious to growth. The great change in teaching will have to come in the area of method, because when the method is right the right things will be learned. (114)

CHAPTER 14

The Next Development In Man

No man is an Iland, intire of itselfe; every man is a peece of the Continent, a part of the maine; if a clod bee washed away by the sea, Europe is the lesse, as well as if a Promontorie were, as well as if a Mannor of thy friends or of thine own were; any man's death diminishes me, because I am involved in Mankinde; and therefore never send to know for whom the bell tolls; it tolls for thee.

—John Donne

The history of man is long, and he has passed through many stages in his development. For the most part these stages have been liberating in their nature. While each development has increased the freedom of man, it has also increased his responsibility. As his freedom has increased, his hazard has become greater. These changes or stages have been slow in coming, and far apart. It was a long span between the time when man invented the wheel, to take some of the load from his back, and his invention of something to propel the wheel. (115)

Since man is an embodiment of energy, the invention of ways to create, control, and use energy other than his own has had a profound effect on the speed of his change. The tempo of change has been enormously stepped up. If we consider what changes have occurred in the condition of man during the flash of time since the invention of the steam engine, we can see that the next development will not be a matter of thousands or millions of years, as the others have been. Decades now take the place of millennia. (116)

We consider this development a proper topic to include in a book on education because it is through education that we can learn how to live with the forces and people that make up life. Whatever we are in attitude and function is learned. Fitness for any new relationship will have to be learned. When we see a fruitful line of development for man we can teach in this direction.

There are those who do not believe that the human race has any future, that it is about to destroy itself. This, to be sure, may be true. It seems likely that the twentieth century is the most critical one in the history of man. It started at a slow tempo. Since not even the automobile had then come into general use, life in 1900 was not greatly different from that in 1800. Now, in the middle of the century, we have acquired the means to destroy ourselves without having gained the attitudes and understandings to keep us from doing so. So far in this century it is touch and go. A dangerous power has been brought into existence, and it is in the hands of a people not yet developed enough to make it safe. Viewed from the mid-point, it seems likely that by the time the century is over we will either have destroyed ourselves or learned how to manage ourselves and our power. The sinister possibilities of atomic fission do not give us the leisure of a thousand years to make a change. (117)

We (the authors) are, however, optimistic about the future of mankind. We cannot fail to realize and to admit that before the needed changes can take place none of us may be here. But the human organism has to be optimistic by its very nature. This is a requirement if the organism is purposive. Purpose implies striving, and striving implies not only survival but also improvement of the condition under which the organism exists. Optimism as ordinarily defined cannot exist in organisms incapable of conscious thought, but all purpose in all living tissue implies improvement, faith, and hope. It is only in man that these feelings can be brought into consciousness. Optimism seems to make sense, and the pessimist is denying the logic of his own purposive nature. At any rate, for the race to destroy itself seems an unsuitable ending to the greatest of all dramas. (118)

We have posed two alternatives for the year 2000: that we learn how to live together or that we destroy ourselves. Our optimism rules out one of these, and leaves the other.

In man's next development he will come to see the unitary principle in all life and in all things. He will see that man and his environment are one—that there is an interaction in which man makes his environment and it makes him. This is the "transaction of living" about which John Dewey has written and said so much, and which Adelbert Ames demonstrates in his laboratory.

When we couple the fact of this interaction with the realization that the only really important thing in environment is other people we can see what other people mean to us, and realize our mandate in regard to them. Life is social, or it is nothing. No human being ever grew into anything but a monstrosity in the absence of other human beings. Our own quality, then, depends upon the quality of the people out of whom we are built. (119)

Thus, we can see that adequate, decent human relations become not just something which is nice to have but a necessity for our own development. If we do not have people of quality around us, we will not have good stuff for our own growth. When we act to reduce or degrade others we reduce or degrade ourselves. (120)

The reason why man behaves so badly now is that he is in the naïve stage of his development. We have pointed out that the basic method of progress for all living things is cooperation, or perhaps what Sinnott calls organization. None of the lower animals or plants possesses consciousness in the same sense that man does. They are, therefore, not able to think about what way of life would be best for them. Not having the capacity to think about it, they behave in accordance with their unconscious purposes. (121)

It comes about that the only creature with the power of choice through conscious thought is the only one which consistently and systematically preys upon its own kind! (122)

When one thinks about one's own enhancement, as all of us must, the naïve view is to grab everything we can for ourselves, getting as far away from others as we can, reducing others through devices in degradation to a degree that they will not threaten us. Among nations, such conduct calls for economic sanctions in one form or another against other peoples, and sanctions often lead to war. When our methods reach the stage of war, one side kills so many of the other side that the latter can no longer carry on, and then the cycle starts over. The basic optimism of the human spirit is probably all that prevents mass suicide on the part of the survivors on the losing side, for the road to successful competition with the victors is so long as to be quite hopeless during the lifetime of any adult individual.

We have to achieve conscious thought before we can think to be naïve. We have to pass through the naïve stage before we can become truly intelligent. Now, in the middle of the twentieth century, we seem to be in that stage. Man is naïve when he thinks he can go forward without others, and when he thinks he can profit in the long run by behavior detrimental to others. While this idea is by no means new, we can set it down as a scientifically demonstrable fact, because of what we now know about the social demands of the organism. (123)

Because of the relationship between man and his environment where each builds the other, we can end our confusion about what is selfish. Enlightened self-interest and selflessness become the same. When the individual acts in full realization of his own need of others he enhances the other in his own behalf. The man who does not see his need for others, but thinks he can proceed to the detriment of others (the naïve view), destroys what he feeds on. We still have the problem of ego enhancement and defense. We all need a place, we need to have respect and to be something of a factor. We can now see how these needs can best be achieved and why they must be achieved.

The establishment of democracy as a way of life and its implementation through governmental devices have been greatly hampered by the naïve concept of self and of others. The democratic ideal requires us to hold that all individuals have unique worth, that all are equal before the law that has been enacted by their consent, and that all have a right to share in the goods of the earth. Freedom within the social framework is implied. The naïve notion that each can best look out for himself, to the detriment of others, denies these ideals. Hence, democracy has had a hard road to travel in establishing itself as a way of life among men. We all know the ideals of democracy, but they do not fit the method of progress that we have been taught. These contradictions not only cause disorganization in our own thinking and acting, but they cause the so-called democracies to present a sorry spectacle to the rest of the world.

Democracy has not yet been tried on a large scale as a way of life. We will have to try it soon. If the human race can survive this critical time, however, democracy is certain to come about. This is because it is the only way that has human freedom at its base. Man has always struggled for freedom, and always will, because this struggling is the only behavior consistent with his purposive nature.

Totalitarian regimes have never survived. They are always overthrown because they deny freedom to purposive organisms. This overthrow often takes too long to be of comfort to individuals who are under the lash, and they die before the event. The contriving for freedom has never ceased since the dawn of the history of man, nor will it cease, because it is consistent with man's nature. This is why authoritarianism carries the seed of its own destruction. It is the reason why we do not need to indoctrinate for democracy. We need to indoctrinate only for those ideas which will not stand up when man behaves in keeping with his basic structure. Authoritarianism is likewise doomed in the home, in the school, and in the church; if this is not true, then we are all doomed.

The old conflict between science and religion no longer needs to persist. From the beginning it should have been clear to us that science and religion could not be in basic conflict. What we are now learning from science with regard to what our relationships must be reveals the verity of the teachings we have had from great religious leaders and from many others who are not called religious leaders but who have spoken to us intuitively. The language of the poet has, in many cases, come to be the language of the scientist, and the relationship between the two is now coming to be understood. We can see now that there has been something basic, down the ages, in what the religious leaders and poets have been teaching us. The reason these teachings have survived is because they fitted human need.

Religion as faith meets a great need for the human organism as it contrives toward freedom. Faith is closely related to purpose and to assumption. We have no directive for the present except our expectation for the future. It is understandable that this expectation extend beyond our so-called mortal lives. This expectation or faith gives sense to purpose and contriving. When religion slips over from faith to ritual and dogma it has a tendency to depart from its basic usefulness. It then lends itself to authoritarianism and tends to lose its function as a reason for behavior. When religion becomes ritual and dogma it is possible for one to take it as one takes a bath; it does not affect behavior. Faith, confidence, expectation have effects on behavior. Ritual and dogma are perversions of what starts as faith. They can be indulged in without regard to behavior. The implications for organized religion are clear.

Were there time and space, it would be interesting to take a large number of the great religious teachings and reinterpret them in relation to the unifying principle of man and his environment, or to the transaction of living. It would reveal the necessity for doing unto others as we would that they do unto us; why it is that as ye do unto the least of these ye do it unto me. We have through this an answer to the old question "Am I my brother's keeper?" Since I am built out of the quality of my brother, and since I cannot be better than the stuff of which I am built, I had better be my brother's keeper, cherishing him as I cherish myself. (124)

If we really believed that we are built out of other people and that our quality depends upon theirs, we would not tolerate the present condition of man, which too often is one of poverty, hunger, and sickness. We permit these conditions because we really do not care, and we do not care because we do not understand. If we did understand, we would face the problem of production and distribution. We would not want to have so much of the goods of earth for ourselves that others could not have enough. We would be willing to forego some of our minor physical comforts for the larger gain of a competent human race, living in peace, on which to feed. Our sacrifices would be but temporary, since a competent human race would greatly increase production. The material loss we suffer through the inability of the starved and the sick to produce is probably our most profligate indulgence.

So-called "good" people—intellectual people—give lip service to the brotherhood of man. They go to meetings where they talk about the unfortunates. They decry the fact that Negroes, for example, are second-class citizens who have to live in slums and have to work at menial tasks for low pay. But little ever happens to alleviate the conditions they decry. One cannot help being impelled to believe that these people really do not care on the doing level. Regardless of our verbal expressions, we cannot avoid assuming that we think we can go forward with large numbers of deprived people in the world, and save most of the goods of the earth for ourselves.

It will not be possible to discuss here all the symptoms of our society which indicate that we are in the naïve stage nor to state what changes in practice will come about through plain logic when we get over this stage. A few can be mentioned briefly:

We will modify our attitudes toward boundaries and barriers. National boundaries were created for exclusion and for defense. They have been considered necessary because peoples everywhere feared the predatory nature of other peoples. Even without any change in attitude, the airplane and the rocket have wiped these boundaries out. But when all men value other men as their most important asset, the idea of exclusion will tend to disappear. Human beings, on the whole, are assets, else there would be no value in humanity. When they come to be so held, the exclusion of assets will cease to make sense.

One of the chief instruments of boundaries is the world's diplomatic corps. The so-called diplomats seldom enter a conference in order to see how a problem may be solved to mutual advantage. Their approach to any problem is that of seeking to get the best of a bargain, to increase the economic status of their own people to the detriment of others. They rarely tell the truth, but use doubletalk, so that no one will know for sure what they mean. The word "diplomacy" is actually changing meaning, so that it is coming to mean evasion. The diplomats are of course not to be blamed personally for this type of action. They are representing their countries in ways required of them by their people. Most of such diplomatic discussions end in stalemates, and must so end from their very nature. (125)

Diplomats are also the chief instrumentality of sovereignty. Sovereignty means the right to do as one pleases within one's own boundary. It therefore tends to solidify boundaries. It is difficult to see how anyone can defend his right to do as he pleases behind his own boundary when any act anywhere now affects the lives of people all over the world.

When man comes to value man, there will be a reduction in personal psychological barriers between people. These barriers are essential to the integrity of the individual, but they get to be too high and too thick so that, in addition to preserving the person as an individual, they serve to exclude other people to the extent that the personality within the barrier starves. When we come to know that other people are what we feed on experientially we will open ourselves so that we can be fed. The barriers we need at one stage in our lives become the vice of our full development. Prejudices thrive within people who exclude people and ideas. People who are open—and they can be open only when they see value in so being—cannot harbor prejudices, for the prejudices become illogical. (126)

What has been said concerning diplomats is true also of group interaction within boundaries. The representatives of management and labor seldom come together to see how problems can be solved to mutual advantage. Each approaches "mediation" with the idea of getting the better of the other. Each sees the other as knavish. Conflict takes the place of mediation, and it is not infrequent that both lose. This example could be illustrated from our society in many ways.

When we come to see man as an asset we will have an end to the notion of retribution. Our whole penal code and many of our educational practices are based on the notion that one can, and should, pay for one's sins. People are sent to jail not to make them better people but to "get even" with them for what they have done. The worse the conditions in jail the "more even" we think we can get. The human being thus incarcerated becomes less and less fit to assume his place in society and, when released, is more of a menace than when he went in. When we abandon the concept of retribution we will substitute the concept of reconstruction. We will need to isolate certain individuals from society, but it will be with a view to giving them a life which will reconstruct them, rather than one which will make their suffering commensurate with their wrongdoing. Some will have to be isolated for life because of our inability to reconstruct them, but not because we think it takes them that long to pay. We will have fewer and fewer of the unreconstructed as we learn better how to live together. Abandonment of the concept of retribution will remake our schools, churches, and homes.

We would see an end to arrogance. While what has been said applies to all peoples of the world, this idea is especially apropos to Americans. Arrogance is a feeling of superiority designed to drive other people away from us. It is a false and harmful notion of virtue. It is particularly virulent in the United States, and accounts for much of the ill will that we have accumulated for ourselves. Arrogance is a symptom of pseudo superiority, because if virtue is genuine it does not need to repel people.

All of this probably sounds moralistic and impractical. It sounds like another preachment such as we have had for thousands of years without greatly improving man's relationship to his fellows. We can hear people say that it is just some more idealism, that it is fine but will not work. Some will say, "Oh, well, you want Utopia!" or, "Let's be realistic!" Others will say it is "soft" while life is hard.

The chief reason why we believe that in the next fifty years man will come to value his fellow, although he has not done so in his long history, is that he will have to do so or perish. His present method of operation is untenable because of the forces of destruction that have been released. When adjustments necessary for survival have confronted man, he has always made them. A change which ordinarily would have taken a long time must now be made quickly. The tempo of living has been so stepped up in this century that the next fifty years will be more than an ordinary millennium.

The common people are more ready to hold a peaceful attitude toward all peoples than is usually realized. They have taken an awful beating in the first half of this century. Millions of them have known personal bereavement from organized violence, and they are asking why this violence needs to go on. They still carry around a baggage of prejudice concerning people who are different from them, but they are willing to sacrifice in order to have a peaceful world. This applies, we believe, to the common people of every land. At the end of World War II we were almost persuaded to abandon our bloodthirsty ways, but then we became frightened, and we have been behaving as frightened people do. Americans became frightened of the Russians. We do not know how much of Russia's behavior since the war has been dictated by fear. But when people fear they soon hate; hatred carries with it the will to destroy. It may be that the peoples of the world will have to take another beating, more terrible than any that has gone before, in order that they may be convinced of the futility of this method of operation. Attitudes tenable for peace are now in the hearts of more people than we can presently realize. These attitudes can eventually affect the way their governmental representatives behave. It is what John Dewey refers to when he says, "The belated revolution which will enable mankind to realize on the potentials of the industrial and political revolutions has still to take place." We have not yet realized on the industrial revolution because so far it probably has added to, rather than diminished, man's misery. It has robbed him of his serenity.

We wish we could say that the change will come because we now have scientific bases by which man can value his fellows. We do have the scientific bases; it is no longer in the realm of opinion or of intuition as it has been for so long. Unfortunately, however, man does not begin to behave better simply because he knows better. He begins to behave better when he gets into a spot where his previous behavior will not serve him. This is the adjustment that has been going on, we believe, in the hearts of the common people. Their revolution has already begun, largely induced by their vicissitudes. Scientific knowledge in support of this change will be helpful. It will give some people a basis for behavior in which they can have confidence. It will stand as a bulwark when predatory people seek to push their own prejudices. Knowledge alone, however, cannot control attitude.

Democracy and all it implies is not soft and easy. If it were, we would long since have tried it. There is no sterner discipline than that which controls one when one realizes that he is responsible to his fellows. Autocrats can be cheated, but a man cannot cheat his fellows and retain his status; nor can he continue to cheat himself. A hard fact of life is that he needs others, and must behave in a manner that will establish and retain rapport with them.

It is only when he does not know his need for others that he thinks he can afford to be undisciplined. All autocrats, and particularly autocratic teachers, who think the democratic way is soft and easy are invited to try it.

As for Utopia—we are in favor of it. Any state of human affairs where people live together in peace and happiness looks good. We are not too sure just what is in the minds of those who accusingly say, "Oh, you want Utopia!" Do they enjoy human misery, and feed upon man's inability, so far, to work out a tenable way of life?

We need to examine the validity of those who say, "Let's be realistic," or, "That's idealistic." There are too many of them to be ignored. Many times when an idea is advanced, it is objected to because it is an idea and, therefore, must be impractical.

Ideas are as practical as concrete sidewalks. Everything that exists in a material way existed first as an idea. The reason why man is able to direct his own evolvement is that he is the only creature gifted with the capacity to imagine. He projects beyond present circumstances, and then acts in order to bring his imagining into concreteness. Not every idea "pans out," to be sure, but there is never any way to know whether it will or not until it is tried. Therefore, no idea can be criticized as impractical until it has been tried. Those of us who are especially gifted in imagination are the ones who account for most of our material advancement. Those who launch themselves into action without having first imagined (had an idea) are the impractical ones. We see them fumbling and failing wherever we look.

Whatever we have exists first as an idea. When the idea is acted upon, it attains "thingness." Its reality or practicality is a result of action. Its final test is determined by the way it functions. It is a whole, from the idea to the use. To say that an idea is impractical is as sensible as to complain about a bulb because it is not a bloom. To try to avoid the idea stage is like trying to have tulips without bulbs. (127)

The place of the school in man's coming to understand his proper relationship to his fellows is a crucial one. Whatever one *is* in functioning attitude has been learned. It is as easy for a child to learn tenable ways as it is for him to learn untenable ones. The isolated person has learned to be isolated. The school is our chief instrument for teaching attitudes and relationships which will work. Mankind could be made over by our educational institutions if learning proper relationships became as important as learning to multiply or to spell. (128)

Our teachers may think they can teach positive attitudes by telling children what to do. We have long had great faith in the value of telling, in spite of the fact that our results in terms of behavior have been disappointing. The way in which proper relationships can be taught is by living those relationships when we come in contact with those whom we would teach. Children will actually learn from the way we act, rather than from what we say. If all we get from the teacher is more preaching about right and wrong, the schools will fail to fulfill their role in working out ways for better living. (129)

The realization of a workable relationship among the peoples of the world is now in the idea stage. Its progress will depend much upon our schools as the prime agents of learning. The idea is supported both by the great teachers of the past and by the science of the present. It is further supported by great need, as shown by the present condition of a war-torn, inhuman world. Man is now ripe for his next development. (130)

We have optimism—it being inherent in purposive organisms. We do not believe that the ultimate destruction or degradation of mankind will occur. We think that the freedom of man can and will be achieved.

We now have the tools with which to work. We have a great institution suited to the task, which, if it did not exist, would be hard indeed to create. We have knowings which we did not have before, and a readiness on the part of people which has been acquired at enormous cost. We are ready now for the first time to reach out and grasp civilization. (131)

PART THREE

The Problem Of Evidence

Education is not a science in its own right. It is doubtful if it ever can be. Much scientific investigation depends for its validity upon matched groups differently treated. The uniqueness of human individuals precludes this technique, or, at best, we only approximate it.

The practice of education, like the practice of medicine, is an applied science. It draws the truths it applies from different disciplines. Many of the truths used by teachers are proved, or could be proved, in the disciplines in which they arise. The advancement of scientific knowledge has outrun its application in education. Often practices are employed which have been invalidated at their source.

It has been the purpose of the authors to bring together in this book such items as have been recently discovered or validated into a kind of article of faith. They constitute a framework within which any re-evaluation or reconstruction of educational theory or practice will need to conform. This condition does not differ from that in which the engineer operates when he plans a bridge, a roadway, or a building. He must operate within the conditions of his task and under the laws that govern his materials.

The assembly and definition of this body of fact have been done in Part One. In Part Two we have undertaken to present the implications of these facts for education. The facts that have been presented form a foundation for an educational philosophy. They serve as criteria for judging present practices. They furnish guideposts for new planning.

In Part Three we cite the sources of our facts and the bases for our beliefs. This section may not interest all readers. It will indicate to such as are curious enough to read it how we came by our values, and why both authors separately, in different books, have

169

described methods which they believe are consistent with the findings.

To those who continue to read, the authors wish to say that the items presented are drawn from laboratory-established materials as far as these are available. Like any other plotters of new paths, we should have liked to have had all the facts. We do not have them. In some areas no studies have yet been made. In other areas the material is so abundant that it is impossible to have covered it all. Life even in the classroom demands action. One has to do whether all the facts are in or not. In teaching, perhaps more than in some other activities, decisions which can be momentous to the life of the learner have to be made in areas where facts are hard to come by.

We need to consider whose words we are willing to accept, and are free to accept and use. Acceptance of fact on authority alone is precarious business unless we differentiate between those who know and those who propagandize. The world is full of people who make statements and get them printed. Sometimes they do this because they just like to make noise, but often they have goals which are harmful to others. Teaching children in school the capacity to differentiate between the propagandist and the one who knows is one of our primary tasks.

Any investigator, however, who would be scientific has to accept the statement of others, because he cannot possibly verify the statements himself. The point of the original research was in part to put the findings on paper so that others could short-cut the research. Nearly all progress depends upon the acceptance of statements by people who know, because finding out cannot and need not be repeated each time.

It probably reduces itself to a matter of respect. When a scientist is known to be accurate, careful, and truthful, and has spent much time in investigation, we accept what he has to say in the field of his investigation. It is not greatly different from life in general. We believe people who talk about things of which they have some knowledge, and who have established a reputation for telling the truth. A friend of ours once said, in discussing this problem, "These things are not true because Jesus said them, but Jesus said them because they are true."

We wish to reiterate here that neither the facts cited nor the implications made are the product of our own imaginations, to support our own theories. Neither are they generalizations based solely on our own experience in lifetimes devoted to teaching. They are facts established by experts, and largely such as may be re-established by any competent investigator. Where such data are lacking we have had recourse to logical hypotheses based upon known facts. There is nonetheless a large area of human concern which does not lend itself to laboratory investigation by any methods now known to us. It is an area acknowledged by tough-minded scientists. Sinnott says: "If there arises in living stuff a goal, an image, longing—call it what you will—which comes to expression in a noble deed, or a great poem, or a new insight into nature, does it not tell us something more profound than present scientific knowledge can do about that remarkable process which at its lowest level goes by the prosaic name of biological organization? The biochemist can tell us much about protoplasmic organization, but so can the artist. Life is the business of the poet as well as the physiologist." A host of other scientists—Planck, Schröd-inger, Cannon, Cassirer, du Nouÿ, Thompson, and Whyte—testify to the significance of the things of the spirit in ethical and aesthetic values, in aspirations and goals.

When life demands action and neither facts nor hypotheses are available, the actor uses what he can get. We obey our intuitions. We play our hunches. We invoke what we call chance. In areas occupied by the affairs of humankind teachers and others are often faced with such situations. Folk knowing, fables, proverbs are the repository of such partial but crucial knowings. The acknowledged insight of the poet has often pointed beyond science, and presaged it. The reader of Part Three will find interspersed with laboratory fact proverbs, bits of poetic insight, fable, and myth.

The reader may be interested in the organization we used to clarify our own thinking. We felt that the hazard of not yet established facts was great but the danger lay less in the data themselves than in a confusion of guess with fact. We have appraised our material in five classifications. We ask ourselves, in determining classifications:

Fact

Can any competent investigator repeat the conditions from which the item rose?

Hypothesis

Does the deduction made from established facts show logical sequence?

Expert Opinion

Has a specialist in any given field projected a fact which may be demonstrable to the uniquely experienced, but not amenable to proof for the inexpert?

Intuition

Has a uniquely experienced person brought up from the depths of self a fact, the bases for which either lie below specific recall or are attributable to extrasensory perception?

Folk Knowing

Has the cumulative experience of the species precipitated certain knowings out of the vast fluid of its experience, which are laid down in proverb, folklore, and fable? Do not these, least reliable because of their fragmentary nature, lie deep in the psychological structure?

But beyond this, the investigator who lacks even such grains of knowing is often called upon to act. Then he must go forward on the faith that is in him, sharing the advice of one Ibsen character to another: "Go forward blindly, trusting the light to find you out."

1. Howard Mumford Jones wrote a book called *Education and World Tragedy*. In it he has brought together some amazing facts about war and the twentieth century. The book was published by the Harvard University Press in 1946. Since then events have indicated the facts were not overdrawn and that the facts there cited were justifiable. He says on page 9: "If the entire population of the United States were wiped out tomorrow, their number would be less than the number of human beings who have died of violence or starvation in war or as the result of it during the last half-century." He also quotes from an article by Pitirim Sorokin: "Professor Pitirim Sorokin estimates that during the first third of this century Europe suffered twenty-four million war casualties

. . . From the eleventh to the twentieth centuries war casualties totaled about fifteen millions. In the first three decades of the present century we have killed $33\frac{1}{3}\%$ more human beings than were killed in the previous eight hundred years. But these figures do not include five other continents and they take us only to the rise of Hitler."

2. Stirred by the dropping of the atomic bomb, Norman Cousins, editor of the *Saturday Review of Literature,* expanded a brief editorial into a small book. It was published by the Viking Press in 1945 under the title of *Modern Man Is Obsolete.* On page 45 Cousins writes: "For though world government provides a better method and a better chance of preserving world peace than man has ever possessed, it cannot provide a guarantee for world peace. It provides man with time—time to think, time to change, time to keep decisions in his own hands, but it cannot make the right decisions for him. It provides only the minimum and not the maximum requirements of a common security. It provides the broad and solid ground in which to sink the foundations of a genuine sovereignty, and on which to build a floor under tomorrow; but it does not provide a finished structure. It provides the form but not the substance. That finished structure and that substance can be provided only by the vision and the day-by-day wisdom of man himself."

3. Julian Huxley published some years ago in the *Yale Review* an essay called "The Uniqueness of Man." Later it appeared in a book of essays published by the Mentor Books. Huxley brings to bear upon the problems of humanity a deep insight and a great competency in the field of science. On page 9 he says: "In the perspective of evolution, tradition and tools are the characters which have given man his dominant position among organisms. This biological dominance is, at present, another of man's unique properties . . . usually at any one time there is one such type—the placental mammals, for instance in the Cenozoic Epoch, but sometimes there are more than one . . . in earlier periods we should be hard put to it to decide whether trilobites, nautiloids or early fish were *the* dominant type. Today, however, there is general agreement that man is the sole type meriting the title."

4. In the foreword of a book by Jackette and Christopher

Hawks, called *Prehistoric Britain,* published first by Penguin Books in 1943, and again in 1946, these authors say succinctly what other anthropologists and archaeologists discuss in detail. On page 11 they say: "Archeology has enabled us to understand how from the moment when primitive human creatures shaped the first tools, chapter after chapter has been added to the tale of man's accomplishments. He masters fire, he discovers a mechanical principle, he becomes an artist, he learns to farm, to weave, to shape pots, to sail boats, to make wheels, to cast bronze, to work iron, until imperceptibly we have reached the unfinished chapter of tomorrow."

5. Andras Angyal, M.D., wrote in 1941 *Foundations for a Science of Personality,* published by the Commonwealth Fund. On page 168 he says: "The human individual, besides its general phylogenetic integration, is a member of a family, a member of a social group, a participant in a culture, a part of nature, and, in the broadest sense, a part of a cosmic order. Thus a person does not lead a purely individual life, but also a family life, a social life, a cultural life, in which he participates and which he shares with others."

6. Ernst Cassirer wrote in 1944 *An Essay on Man,* published by the Yale University Press. On page 5 he says: "We cannot discover the nature of man in the same way that we can detect the nature of physical things. . . . For it is only in our immediate intercourse with human beings that we have insight into the character of man."

7. Julian Huxley includes in *Man in the Modern World,* published by Harper & Brothers, 1927, an interesting essay entitled "The Intelligence of Birds." In it he discusses some interesting data about the quick changes birds make from one state of being to another. The bird that has had eggs substituted for a nest of young, hesitates only briefly, then takes up the task where she finds it. More exactly, she releases the instinctive energy roused by the stimulus in instinctive response. He closes the article on page 110 with the sentence: "We, whether we want to or not, cannot help living in the framework of a continuing life. Our powers of thought and imagination bind up the present with the future and the past; the bird's life is almost wholly a patchwork, a series of self-sufficing moments."

8. Edmund W. Sinnott wrote *Cell and Psyche,* published by the University of North Carolina Press in 1950. On page 100 he says: "Man has climbed the age-old evolutionary stairway from its simplest beginnings. In this progress the organized living system in which successively his ancestral life was passed became more complex, and the outreach of his mind and spirit grew ever wider. A strange paradox of nature is the contrast between this constant upward thrust in the evolution of life and the downward drift of all lifeless nature as pictured by the second Law of Thermodynamics."

9. Sir D'arcy W. Thompson, the great English biologist, wrote a momumental book, *Growth and Form.* It was published by the Cambridge University Press in 1948. Its more than one thousand pages are devoted to the minute study of growth and the forms it takes on hundreds of levels. He says, on page 13: "How far even mathematics will suffice to describe, and physics to explain, the fabric of the body, no man can foresee. It may be that all the law of energy, and all properties of matter, and all the chemistry of all the colloids are as powerless to explain the body as they are impotent to comprehend the soul. For my part, I think it is not so. Of how it is that the soul informs the body, physical science teaches me nothing; and that living matter influences and is influenced by mind is a mystery without a clue. Consciousness is not explained to my comprehension by all the nerve paths and neurones of the physiologist; nor do I ask of physics how goodness shines in one man's face, and evil betrays itself in another. But of the structure and growth and working of the body, as of all else of the earth, physical science is in my humble opinion our only teacher and guide."

10. Sinnott, *Cell and Psyche,* page 19: "Protoplasm is a bridge anchored at one end in the simple stuff of chemistry and physics, but at the other reaching far across into the mysterious dominions of the spirit."

11. Lecomte du Nouÿ wrote *Human Destiny,* published by Longman, Green in 1947. On page 136 he says: "Our body makes us an integral part of that colossal evolutive current of life which shrank, little by little, until it was reduced to the human strain, but by our moral and spiritual ideas we are related to the perfect

being toward which evolution has tended since the beginning. On the one side we are linked to all the beings which preceded. On the other side we are the ancestors of a race which will be infinitely superior to us and which will seek to liberate itself from us as a chick seeks to leave its shell."

12. Sinnott, *Cell and Psyche*, page 13: "It is not, of course, the problems of theoretical biology as such which chiefly interest man or are significant for his welfare, but the higher aspects of man's life emerge from these. Such are problems of biology in its broad sense but of biology at a much higher level than that of the laboratory. If we can bring these loftier matters down to their common protoplasmic denominator and find some problem which is basic to all of them, we shall help to clarify the great objectives which we seek and to bring unity to the search."

13. Irwin Schrödinger, *What Is Life* (Macmillan, 1945): "Freedom is characteristic of living things."

14. Sinnott, *Cell and Psyche,* page 87: "Such obstacles to it [purpose] and to us, are often too powerful and prevent the attainment of an end. But this sort of bondage we recognize as such. It does not destroy our belief that we are really free, for it does not affect the fundamental mechanism through which purpose is translated into deed. This translation is clearly part of the same dynamic system as the setting up of the purpose itself. . . . It is we who will and do, not some agent foreign to us. Surely, if this is so, we do what we will, for the desires which arise in us are an essential part of us, and to speak of compulsion here seems foolish."

15. Dr. Karen Horney wrote in *Our Inner Conflicts* (Norton, 1945), a clear statement of the nature of growth. She says, on page 19: "My own belief is that man has the capacity as well as the desire to develop his potentialities and become a decent human being, and that these deteriorate if his relations to others and hence to himself is, and continues to be disturbed. I believe that man can change and keep on changing as long as he lives."

16. Hadley Cantril has written a book called *The Why of Man's Experience*. It was published by Macmillan in 1950. On page 86 he says: "And so behavior in new situations can be guided only by the value judgments we can make."

17. Thompson, *Growth and Form,* page 20: "Matter as such

produces nothing, changes nothing, does nothing . . . the spermatozoon, the nucleus, the chromosomes or the germ-plasm can never act as matter alone, but only as seats of energy and as centers of force."

18. Lecomte du Nouÿ, *Human Destiny*, page 80: "Memory which is the essential condition for the persistence of living beings, existed in the rudimentary animals; . . . This is certain: evolution could not have taken place without it. The insect is the prisoner of his instincts. The intelligence of mammals expresses the greater liberty acquired through their evolution."

19. The people who speak so glibly of the Law of the Jungle should quote the whole of the passage:

> Now this is the Law of the Jungle
> As old and as true as the sky;
> And the wolf that shall keep it
>   may prosper
> But the wolf that shall break it
>   must die.
> . . . the strength of the pack is the wolf
> and the strength of the wolf is the pack.
>
> —Kipling

20. One of the most remarkable stories of getting on together comes from—of all places—a study on the rearing of small-mouth bass carried on at the Ohio State University. Dr. T. H. Langlois wrote his findings in Bulletin No. 33, Ohio Biological Survey. Langlois, who is the bureau chief, had noticed that bass put into weedy ponds took up residence in secluded places among the weeds. They were unacquainted with each other, and soon became predatory and cannibalistic. So common was this behavior that it was generally believed that small-mouth bass were cannibalistic "by nature." Langlois put young bass into ponds previously cleared of weeds. All fish were fed together. They had to mingle. They became acquainted. When everybody knew everybody and everybody shared common food, nobody tried to eat anybody.

21. W. C. Allee and his coworkers at the University of Chicago have discovered many situations in which mutuality and coopera-

tion are in evidence in a wide range of levels. Goldfish grow better in water where goldfish have been. Worms subjected to lethal irradiation and then segregated do not live as long as the worms left in groups. Grouped worms lived 148 minutes following irradiation. Individually segregated worms lived only 78 minutes. They have also found that tadpoles whose tails had been cut off regenerated faster when other tadpoles were in the tank than when the individuals were alone. Ants move more dirt when they work together than when the same number work alone.

22. Ashley Montagu, professor of anthropology at Rutgers University, says in an article published in *Scientific American*, April, 1950: "In the first weeks of life the human infant appears solely concerned with satisfying its physical needs, such as food and warmth. But gradually its feelings of satisfaction are transferred to the person or persons who make the satisfaction possible. From then on the baby is not content with merely getting enough to eat; it also needs a close emotional connection with the provider —the mother or mother-substitute. It cannot live by bread alone. Thus the mutuality which governs the infant's life in the uterus is raised to the psychic level. The baby now has a 'social inclination.' ". . . "To love thy neighbor as thyself is not only religion's edict but nature's as well."

23. Lecomte du Nouÿ, *Human Destiny*, page 15: "The external world, nature, is revealed to us through our sense organs. We see the stars, the sun, the mountains, the animals, and other men by means of the eye which is constructed like a photographic apparatus. The retina is composed of an immense number of sensitive elements, the so-called rods and cones. The reactions of these elements, are transmitted through the optic nerve to certain brain centers. These reactions are the cause of what we call visual impressions. It is, therefore, not the eye which sees but the brain."

24. Earl C. Kelley has written *Education for What Is Real*, which was published by Harper & Brothers in 1947. After recounting the experiments conducted at the Hanover Institute, the author formulates the laboratory findings: "We do not get our perceptions from the things around us, but that the perceptions come from us. . . . Since the perception is the usable reality, and since no two organisms can make the same use of clues or bring

the same experimental background to bear, no two of us can see alike. We have no common world."

25. Quoted from William H. Kilpatrick concerning his experience with the Hanover Institute demonstrations, created by Adelbert Ames, Jr.: "We who have studied these experiments in the light of broader thinking see other and more important bearings and this along two distinguishable lines. The first line is that the eye process of perception is, as a mere seeing process, of far wider application than appears to the uninitiated. The second line is that the way that the eye in these experiments is shown to act is a characteristic part of human behavior and therefore illustrative of each other line of behavior in the total organism's response; illustrative in fact of human behavior in certain of its most fundamental and inclusive aspects."

26. Two zoology professors of Columbia, L. C. Dunn and T. Dobzansky, have written a book called *Heredity, Race and Society*. It was first published in 1946. In it they say, page 45: "If man has no fewer genes than a Drosophila fly, a human sex cell must carry several thousand genes. Let us assume that only about three hundred of these genes are each represented by at last two alternative conditions such as A and a, dominant and recessive. This is almost certainly an underestimate but for the purposes of the argument we are going to make an underestimate as preferable to an overestimate. Three hundred gene differences are capable of producing a fantastic number of combinations—more than there are electrons and protons in the universe. Although we cannot as yet make an exact count of human genes, we can be very sure that all the gene combinations which exist in all the humans living in the world constitute just a negligible fraction of the gene combinations that could be formed." . . . . "The chance that any two human beings, now living or having lived have identical sets of genes is practically zero, identical twins always excepted."

27. Alfred Korzybski wrote *Science and Sanity*, an introduction to non-Aristotelian systems and general semantics. It was published by the Science Press, in 1927. On page 374 he says: "Again the reports received through particular channels are influenced by the kind of reports that have already come through those channels. To one who has not seen trees frequently, a spruce

and a balsam are not seen to be different. They are just 'evergreens.' With better educated seeing, this individual later differentiates perhaps four kinds of spruce. Because of this factor of experience, the response of each individual to similar external stimuli is individual."

28. Karen Horney has written a book called *Neurosis and Human Growth*. It was published by Norton in 1950. Dr. Horney is a psychiatrist, and her examples are drawn from her work with patients. "The essence of these remarkable matters is significant to all people who, in the process of their growth, have made one-sided judgments of their motivations or have seen themselves 'through a glass darkly.' "

29. On page 34, in speaking of self-knowledge, she says:"The road of analytical therapy is an old one, advocated time and again throughout human history. In the terms of Socrates and the Hindu philosophy, among others, it is the road to reorientation through self-knowledge."

30. Dr. Horney has also written *Self-Analysis,* published by Norton in 1942. On page 36 she says: "Certain gains are beckoning to those who are capable of self-analysis which are more spiritual in character, less tangible but not less real. These gains can be summarized as an increase of inner strength and therefore of self-confidence. Every successful analysis increases self-confidence, but there is a certain extra gain in having conquered territory entirely through one's own initiative, courage and perseverance. This effect is the same in analysis as in other areas of life. To find a mountain path all by one's self gives a greater feeling of strength than to take a path that is shown, though the work put in is the same and the result is the same. Such achievement gives rise not only to a justifiable pride but also to a well-founded feeling of confidence in one's capacity to meet predicaments and not feel lost without guidance."

31. Sinnott, *Cell and Psyche,* quotes the zoologist E. S. Russell on page 45: "The fact is that the common ground of both organic and psychological activity lies in the directiveness or 'drive' which is characteristic of both. We must regard directiveness as an attribute not of mind but of life. . . . Purposive activity, as seen in its

highly developed form in the intelligent behavior of man, is a specialized and elaborated kind of directive activity, concerned mainly with the mastery of his material environment."

32. Sinnott, *Cell and Psyche,* page 108: "But if we can set these problems up against the background of life itself, if we can show that mind and body, spirit and matter, are held together in equal union as parts of that organized system which life is, then the idealist is encouraged to speak with much more confident voice. He can claim with assurance that mind is as real as body, for they are part of the same unity; that purpose and freedom are not illusions but are an essential part of the way in which events are brought to pass in protoplasmic systems; that the soul has a sound biological basis as the core of the integrated living organism; that our sense of values is not arbitrary, but results from the directions and preferences shown by such systems; and that the course and history of life, so different from those of lifeless matter, give hope that it may have an inner directive quality of its own."

33. L. L. Whyte wrote *The Unitary Principle in Physics and Biology.* It was published by Henry Holt and Company in 1949. On page 99 he says: "All the general properties of organisms are implicit in the unitary principle but exceptional conditions are necessary to render them explicit in actual processes. There is a bias toward order in the unitary principle; in certain circumstances this leads to crystalline symmetry, in others to biological organization."

34.   Yet all experience is an arch
           Where through gleams the untraveled world,
           Whose margins fade forever and forever
           As I move.

                                                    —Tennyson

35. Sinnott, *Cell and Psyche,* page 80: "A standard, norm, or goal set up in living stuff but still to be reached creates the desire for its attainment; and if this attainment is prevented, or if the equilibrium is thrown off—out of balance, the organism experiences unease, pain, or distress of body or mind."

36. Sinnott, page 97: "Living things are seekers and creators, and striving for goals is the essence of life; but in man these goals

have risen to heights before undreamed of, and he can set them ever-higher at his will. Man's feet are planted in the dust, but he lifts his face to the stars."

37. Sinnott, page 102: "Perhaps life has one great purpose, and the levels we have followed—developmental, physiological, psychological, and spiritual—may be successive stages in its ultimate fulfillment."

38. In an old Austrian folk tale three wayfarers stopped at noon to rest beneath an oak tree. One, looking up through the branches, said, "What a fine mast this oak would make for a ship such as I used to sail upon." A second who had been a draper's assistant, said: "What a fine brown cloth my master could have dyed from this fine bark." The third, who had spent his youth as a swineherd, said: "What fine fat pigs could be grown from the acorns which fall from this oak."

39. It is a generally accepted terminology to differentiate between what appears as purpose on low levels of organization, and even below the usually accepted line between organic and inorganic, and what is called purpose on the conscious level of human thinking. It is usual to label as drives such purposes as seem to lie below the level of those organisms which can order or have ordered their purpose in consciousness, reserving the label "purpose" for the latter. In an attempt to call attention to the directive nature of these drives on low organizational levels, we have chosen to use the term "tissue purposes." These would include those processes executed within the organism by the smooth muscles, the processes of homeostasis, and the like. This arbitrary choice is intended to hold more closely in concept the totality of the process of living matter, from the lowest to the highest reaches. For those to whom this is offensive the term "drive" may be substituted. When Sinnott speaks on page 54 of "the concentration of various dissolved chemical substances in particular cells" he says that "these are essentially the same sort of regulations as in homeostasis but involve no nervous mechanism."

40. Sinnott quotes Sherrington: "We seem to watch battalions of specific catalysts like Maxwell's 'demons,' line up, stop-watch in hand, for its moment to play the part assigned to it, a step in one or another great thousand-link chain of process. . . . The processes

going forward in it are cooperatively harmonized. The total system is organized."

41. Sinnott, page 55: "It is this building to plan which is so characteristic of all life. Such a physiological plan, refined and far more complex in the cells of our nervous systems but essentially like the developmental plan, I believe is that which in man can be experienced as conscious purpose. Its roots are deep in the regulatory behavior of protoplasm. Homeostasis is not simply a curious process in physiology. It is the satisfaction of our most basic desires."

42. Dr. Ashley Montagu has written a volume called *The Human Organism and Reproduction, Heredity and Growth,* published by the Delphian Society in 1949. On page 446 he says: "Since genes are composed of large complex molecules, there is virtually no limit to the possible types of bodily chemical reactions they can enter into. In the same way, the theoretical number of distinct types of proteins, with their own unique properties, the genes can contain is almost limitless."

43. Andras Angyal, *Foundations for a Science of Personality.* In chapter X, he discusses life as a gestalt: Holistic psychology, which is characterized by the recognition of an overall system principle in the evolvement of personality, sees the growth of a personality as a process of perfecting the system principle unique to the organism. Since the vast potentiality of the human organism makes the drive toward perfection relative, then we may define the growth of the individual as the process of becoming ever more perfectly what it already is. The holistic psychologist will label this principle Pregnanz a tendency toward the perfect realization of the system principle.

44. L. L. Whyte wrote *The Next Development in Man.* It was published by Henry Holt and Company in 1948. On page 249 he says: "Man can only understand himself by viewing himself as a system in which a dominant formative process organizes an organic hierarchy of such process in an environment of similar processes."

45. Julian Huxley, *Man in the Modern World,* page 151: "But if the world stuff is both matter and mind in one; if there is no break in continuity between the thinking, feeling of an adult human being, and the inert ovum from which he developed; no break

in continuity between life and not life—why, then, mind or something of the same nature as mind must exist throughout the entire universe."

46. L. L. Whyte, *The Unitary Principle in Physics and Biology*. On page 43 he says: "Thus the aim of unitary science is a logical circle representing man and his ideas as part of a unitary nature, and unitary nature as a valid idea emerging to clarity in man. Man will then understand the laws of nature, and the laws of nature will interpret man to himself."

47. Julian Huxley, *Man in the Modern World*, page 16 *(Mentor Edition)*: "A brain capable of conceptual thought could not have been developed elsewhere than in a human body . . . Speech could never have developed in a solitary type . . . The essential character of man as a dominant organism is conceptual thought. And conceptual thought could have arisen only in a multicellular animal, an animal with bilateral symmetry, and blood system, a vertebrate as against a mollusc or an arthopod, a land vertebrate among vertebrates. Finally it could have arisen only in a mammalian line which was gregarious, which produced one young at birth instead of several, and which had recently become terrestrial after a long period of arboreal life."

48. Ashley Montagu, *The Human Organism*, page 480: "Growth does not proceed at an even tempo. Every organ in the body and every system of organs have their own rate of growth. Each child has his own pattern of growth which may or may not resemble the average pattern. . . .

"Thus we see how heredity and environment work together in affecting growth. While heredity determines what we may do, environment determines what we shall do. An individual who has inherited traits for less than average height will never grow extremely tall. But, if the environment is poor, he may never grow to be as tall as his heredity would permit him to be. In short, while heredity imposes limits upon the potentialities of growth, these limits cannot be reached where the environment is inadequate."

49. Karen Horney, *Neurosis and Human Growth*. She says, on page 17: "Similarly, the human individual, given a chance, tends to develop his particular human potentialities. He will develop, then, the unique alive forces of his real self: the clarity and depth of his own feelings, thoughts, wishes, interests; the ability to tap

his own resources, the strength of his will power; the special capacities or gifts he may have; the faculty to express himself, and to
relate himself to others with his spontaneous feelings. All this will
enable him to find his set of values and his aims in life. In short
he will grow, substantially undiverted, toward self-realization.
And this is why I speak now and throughout the book of the real
self as that central inner force, common to all human beings and
yet unique to each, which is the deep source of growth."

50. Ashley Montagu, *The Human Organism,* page 386: "The
neopallium is one of the reasons for man's uniqueness in the animal
kingdom . . . The neopallium itself receives messages from all the
sensory organs except the sense of smell. Even more important,
the neopallium not only connects sensations but is the seat of memory. Consciousness that has the sense of the past also leads to a
concern for the future." Thus the neopallium not only regulates
and coordinates, but also helps to predict future actions on the
basis of the past and aids us in picking and choosing our goals in
life. The greater the development of the neopallium, the more we
are free from instinctive behavior and the more we can learn from
the past to pick and choose our own actions."

51. Andras Angyal, *Foundations for a Science of Personality,*
page 192: "Culture defines the meaning of objects and of various
forms of behavior and by such definitions lends them positive or
negative values."

52. Stuart Chase wrote *The Tyranny of Words.* It was published in 1938. On page 210 he says: "Language was reduced to an
orderly instrument by the Greeks with rules of grammar. . . . Their
early philosophers regarded words as possessing power in themselves, even as the infant and the conjure man regard them. To
classify, some of them believed, was to name, and the name of a
thing was its soul, its essence. Therefore to know the name was to
have power over the soul."

53. "Now abideth faith, hope and *charity.*" King James Version.
   "Thus faith, hope and *love* live on." Moffatt Translation.
   "As for Charity—we've had enough of Charity—even the
   kind you mean.
      And any way, Charity is a dirty word, it's gone to bed
   Too often with philanthropists . . ."
                                        —Edna St. Vincent Millay

"Wam, bam, ala ka zam,
Love hit me between the eyes."
Popular song, entitled "Orange-Colored Sky."

54. Earl C. Kelley, *Education for What Is Real*, page 34: "Our perceptions do not come simply from the objects around us, but from our past experiences as functioning purposive organisms . . . Because our forecasts usually approximate correctness, we make the mistake of assuming they are perfect, and that we do have a common world. It has been pointed out that without cooperation in free human relations there can be no fusion of the individual knowings. The common world, such as we have, comes about because we have shared our knowings, and thus come nearer to whatever constitutes reality in the items of externality."

55. Karen Horney, *Neurosis and Human Growth,* in her illuminating chapter on "The Tyranny of the Should," points out clearly the evils attendant upon such tyranny. The teacher "should" control the room, handle the difficult, know all the answers. This massive tyranny could make cowards of us all, if once it became our basic motivation.

56. The phrase "put distance between" was much used by Alfred Adler to indicate the way in which the fearful find ways to use even objects like furniture to put actual space between them and their tasks for which they feel inadequate. Every teacher is acquainted with the devices of dropped books and broken or lost pencils employed by children who work under duress. The teachers who can recognize this in their pupils are often unaware that they are using their own desks, their power with punishments and grades, passings and failures, as similar barricades between themselves and their learners.

57. The term 'escape' is used by many to connote the same behavior. The Horney description of the three ways of behavior—to move toward, against, or away—covers this concept in the last of the three. See *Neurosis and Human Growth*.

58. A student known to us seemed as a small child uniquely able with language. Before she was proficient in spelling she often brought paper and pencil to her adults asking them to "make" skate, or whatever word she needed. This flowered consistently

until the seventh grade, where she encountered a teacher who was punitive by nature and prided herself on being tough. On a breath-taking morning when trees and shrubs gleamed with ice, the child said, "Oh, I would like to write this in a poem, but I wouldn't get the semicolons in the right place, I don't suppose." By such as these the schools often do what Dr. Winship so deplored: "We get them in the kindergarten," he said, "exclamation points and question marks. We turn them out from the twelfth grade plain periods."

59. Sinnott, *Cell and Psyche*, page 7: "To understand the means by which thousands of genes—presumably protein molecules—in every cell so guide the chemical activities of protoplasm that an organ is produced, is very difficult. J. S. Haldane went so far as to say that 'the mechanistic theory of heredity is not merely unproven, it is impossible.'"

Page 17: "The nineteenth century produced the magnificent conception of life as dynamic, changing, ever moving forward; of the history of the world as the great stage on which the drama of organic evolution is being enacted. But it also established the equally important conception that life has its physical basis in the remarkable material system which is called protoplasm. Here in this aggregation of proteins—water, formless, and flowing, deceptive in its visible simplicity but amazingly complex in its ultimate organization—are centered all the problems of living things. It is not greatly different chemically and physically in bacterium and orchid, in amoeba, arthopod, and man. Life is protoplasmic activity, and this is essentially the same from protozoan to primate. Man is not only cousin to all living things by blood-relationship, but is built of the very same stuff as they. It is not of dust and clay that we are all made, but of proteins and of nucleic acids."

60. Julian Huxley, *Man in the Modern World*, pages 25-26: "Those of man's unique characteristics which may better be called psychological and social than narrowly biological, spring from one or the other of three characteristics. The first is his capacity for abstract and general thought: the second is the relative unification of his mental processes, as against the much more rigid compartmentalization of animal mind and behavior: the third is the existence of social units, such as tribe, nation, party, and church

with a continuity of their own, based on organized tradition and culture.

"In point of fact, the great majority of man's activities and characteristics are by-products of his primary distinctive characteristics, and therefore, like them biologically unique.

"On the one hand, conversation, organized games, education, sport, paid work, gardening, the theatre; on the other conscience, duty, sin, humiliation, vice, penitence—these are all unique by-products. The trouble, indeed, is to find any human activities which are not unique. Even the fundamental biological attributes such as eating, sleeping, and mating have been tricked out by man with all kinds of unique frills and peculiarities."

61. Excerpt from the report of group work from the Y.M.C.A. Conference in Helsinki, August, 1926, quoted by Harrison S. Elliot in *The Process of Group Thinking*, page 216: "The whole adventure in leadership in such complex groups was new to most of them ... No man however in his own group knew how the things had gone in the other groups ... When, therefore, the leaders came streaming back into the room in the late afternoon for the leader's meeting, from half-past four until six—each fresh from the discussion of his own group, but not knowing a word of what had happened in other groups—the expectancy was tense ... The difficulties were tabulated in their order of importance. The group's views as to what were the causes of the problems were also listed.

"As a result, in an hour and a half, the whole mind of the fifty groups composing the entire conference as expressed in the day's discussion was expressed, and the main outline of its conclusions arranged in as orderly a fashion as the very turmoil and confusion of the thought itself would permit."

Page 221: "Whether discussion and participation are secured by this plan depends upon the person in charge of a particular hour, just as the participation of a class of persons in a college or university class depends upon whether the professor chooses and is able to use this method."

62. Earl C. Kelley, *The Workshop Way of Learning*, page 152: Roland C. Faunce says, "I have thought a number of times that after a semester or a year of the education workshop a kind of

by-product which is clearly evident to me in these people is a liberalizing of their views toward functional education; something which we haven't sought to do as staff members, completely a by-product resulting I think from a greater feeling of comfort, security, etc., in interaction with others. After a semester or year of workshop they are more ready to accept a shocking idea such as Fred [Walcott] reports from research."

63. For a long time research in the fields of attitude, set, and the like suffered from a lack of realization that attitudes are quite different educational product from knowledge items or degrees of skill. They must be differently dealt with, and different criteria must be established for their evaluation. Attitudes, as they relate to value judgments, and thus to the energy release to fulfill purposes, tend to fall in that classification considered by the semanticists as most fundamental, namely, the "unspeakable" level. The researchers who questioned the blind man whom Jesus reportedly healed of his blindness, must also have been baffled at his response: "Whereas I was once blind, I now see."

64. Ashley Montagu, "Social Instincts," *Scientific American,* April, 1950: "Consider a unicellular organism, the amoeba. When the amoeba reaches a certain size, it can avoid death only by dividing . . . Here is a real example of interdependent social life; it exhibits in miniature the pattern of cooperative behavior that we see throughout nature. Cooperation is the mechanism by which every new individual is formed, whether sexually or a-sexually. Cooperation is the means by which it keeps alive through the first precarious stages of existence. Cooperation is as basic to its nature as are irritability and motility."

65. In an unpublished study by one of the authors on children's lies it was discovered that 72 per cent of the lies, told by 6,000 children, were designed to escape punishment which was expected from adults. The next largest percentage fell in what might be called the zero in lying, that is, observations were inaccurately reported, because incompletely understood. The lie classified as "malicious" by the investigator—the one thought to be so damaging that it must be rooted out in early childhood—is a purely adult achievement.

66. The psychological and psychiatric files are full of evidence

that dullness is often changed into brightness with medication, feeding, and secure and warm environment. The records of the opposite are available, but seldom exploited. In a school in which children are constant in their attendance from year to year although it is an underprivileged and segregated group, a large percentage of IQs move consistently down from kindergarten to the eighth grade. There are no degenerative diseases operating upon these brains, except those of restricted living, narrow potentialities for ultimate success, and a too common conviction on the part of teachers that they are "no good and never will be."

67. Some years ago a group of children who were members of an open-air school group heard that their fellows in regular school had report cards. They begged for them, and against the judgment of their teachers were given report cards as an experiment. The day the cards were received every child ran a temperature!

68. Sinnott, *Cell and Psyche,* page 23: "The word organism is one of the happiest in biology, for it emphasizes what is now generally regarded as the most characteristic trait of a living thing, its organization."

69. Stuart Chase, *The Tyranny of Words,* page 231: "When a physicist says that an atom is 'free' he does not mean in this context that Atom is a rugged individualist with a mind of his own prepared to tolerate no nonsense from an interfering government. He means that the motions of atoms are subject to chance."

70. Quoted by Cassirer in *The Problem of Knowledge:* Fustel de Coulanges, *The Ancient State,* Vol. III, page 266: "The ancients knew neither freedom in their private lives, nor freedom in education, nor religious freedom. The person of the individual was of little import compared with the inviolable and almost divine authority claimed by what one called the state, or the fatherland . . . It was believed that morality, justice, the right must all give way before the good of the fatherland. Thus it is the strangest of all errors to believe that in the communities of antiquity a man enjoyed freedom. He did not even possess the idea of it."

71. John Dewey, *Reconstruction of Philosophy,* Mentor, 1950, page 161: "Freedom for an individual means growth, ready change when modification is required."

Page 162: "Personality must be educated, and personality cannot

be educated by confining its operations to technical and specialized things, or to the less important relationships of life. Full education comes only when there is a responsible share on the part of
each person in proportion to capacity, in shaping the aims and
policies of the social groups to which he belongs. This fact fixes
the significance of democracy."

72. Charles Morgan, in his novel called *The Fountain,* allows
a character to quote from an old church father's work, without
giving us its source. A beautiful allegory ends with the sentence,
which cuts clear between freedom and slavery, page 71: "Now I
am in the liberty of His prison."

73.   I shall be glad, I think
     When time has ceased
     And life cries: "columns halt"
     Before the last dim dusty citadel.
     It will be good to know
     That here at last
     Will fall the final blow
     In that eternal draw
     Twixt Life and Death.
     I shall remember how
     So little time ago
     Earth gave me suckle
     As the small roots curled
     Round the soil
     Like baby's lips—
     When being upright only meant
     To reach down root
     And thrust up stalk into the sun.
     I shall remember, too, I think
     The million-egged futility
     Where only one might live.
     When life was prodigal of stuff
     And niggardly of chance to let it grow.
     And now that life thinks more of me
     Than these—
     I scarce know why,
     Can it not be that this last

Desperate mischance
Is little worse
Than these things used to be?
Can I not make of this
Last crucifixion,
Holiday?

—Marie I. Rasey

74. Herbert Muller, quoted by Sinnott, in *Cell and Psyche*, page 45: " 'Purpose' is not imported into nature and need not be puzzled over as strange or divine something else that gets inside and makes things go; it is no more an added force than mind is some thing in addition to brain. It is simply implicit in the fact of organization, and is to be studied rather than admired or 'explained.' "

75. Du Nouÿ, *Human Destiny*, page 151: "Everything takes place as though moral education were a luxury, 'supplementary course' required by habit, but not worth the trouble of adapting either to the intellectual ability of the student or to the transformation undergone by our science and our philosophy in the last fifty years."

Page 176: "On the other hand if the moral law dominates, it will not oppose itself in any way to the free development of the mind. It will progressively gain ground and will allow all the human, intuitive, and intellectual characters to develop in perfect freedom. It will allow the human spirit to blossom and to perfect itself without limit."

76. Ashley Montagu, in an article entitled "Social Instincts," *Scientific American*, April, 1950, says: "Thus we reach the conclusion that the ethical idea of love is no artificial creation of philosophers, but is rooted in the biological structure of man. To love thy neighbor as thyself is not only religion's edict but nature's as well ... through many laboratory experiments and observations in the field we are being shown that we have been close to 100% wrong in thinking of animal life as a dog-eat-dog existence. The truth seems to be that nature adheres to the principles of the highest ethics: the Golden Rule is sound biology."

77. It is an interesting comment upon the situation, that when a first attempt was made to put the ideas of Dewey and Kilpatrick into action, it was necessary for the school people to design furni-

ture for freedom, since no manufacturer had anything which was self-supporting like a table or chairs! Regimentation is still rather the order than the exception.

78. Du Nouÿ, *Human Destiny,* page 154: "Education is the weapon of progress, one of the weapons of evolution; but it has been turned into a personal, national, political lever. Humanity should realize that, within reasonable limits, it must be de-nationalized. Will the nations recognize that the peril through which civilization has just escaped could only attain its gigantic proportions through the schools? . . . Nothing is easier than to exalt racial or national pride, to create a fanatical esprit de corps and to erect a sanquinary idol. A child's virgin mind is an ideal soil for the development of any idea, right or wrong; but he is closer to the oldest and most dangerous tendencies of humanity than the mature mind which has had time to live and to think. Up till now, only the dictators have availed themselves of this elementary observation, and of the power of lies. If truth alone were taught in schools, throughout the world, there could be no totalitarian states. Only through the schools can we undo the harm the schools have done."

79. A. N. Whitehead has written a book called *The Aims of Education.* It was published by Macmillan in 1929. On page 43 he says: "That knowledge which adds greatness to character is knowledge so handled as to transform every phase of immediate experience. It is in respect to the activity of knowledge that over-vigorous discipline is so harmful. The habit of active thought, with freshness, can only be generated by adequate freedom. Undiscriminating discipline defeats its own objects by dulling the mind. If you have much to do with the young as they emerge from the university, you soon note the dulled minds of those whose education has consisted in the acquirement of inert knowledge."

80. Alfred Adler asked his students to distinguish between behavior which was predicated upon illogical data and that which was in actuality illogical. Since energy is released to the muscles for behaving only when a value judgment, freshly made or dependent upon earlier ones, has become habitual, it is obvious that one in whom sequential processes are operative will behave with what is for him logic from his premise. One who runs and

hides at the sound of feet may have a completely logical performance, but it may still be quite illogical that these feet be feared.

81. We have it on the word of no less than Sinnott (*Cell and
Psyche,* Chapter II) and Julian Huxley (*The Uniqueness of Man*)
that organization is the process from protoplasm to conceptual
thinking. When no false barriers are set up to isolate one from
another aspect, all so-called disciplines flow together into a totality
of knowing, and sciences appear as science.

82. The derivation of this many-faceted word, "courage," reveals a basic meaning of heartedness. Surely the feeling of fitness
is closely associated with the actual economy of the tissues. In the
figurative sense in which the heart is often mentioned as the seat
of bravery, deep regard, and the like, courage becomes a word
with a high affective value. It takes on a greater significance when
its opposite, fear, is called into question. Schools of psychiatry
which differ sharply from each other agree rather generally that
fear or anxiety lies at the root of many mental ills, and the degree
of cure may be estimated in terms of the extent to which courage
replaces fear.

83. V. Gordon Childe has written *Man Makes Himself.* It was
published by Watts and Company in 1936. In it he says on page
15: "The wild sheep is fitted for survival in a cold mountain climate by its heavy coat of hair and down. Men can adapt themselves to life in the same environment by making coats out of
sheeps' skin or of wool. With claws and snouts, rabbits can dig
themselves burrows to provide shelter against cold and enemies.
With picks and shovels, man can excavate similar refuges, and
even build better ones of brick, stone and timber. Lions have claws
and teeth with which to secure the meat they need. Man makes
arrow and spears for slaying his game. An innate instinct, an
inherent adjustment of its rudimentary nervous system, enables
even the lowly jelly-fish to grasp prey that is actually within its
reach. Men learn more efficient and discriminating methods of
obtaining nourishment through the precept and example of their
elders."

"In human history, clothing, tools, weapons, and tradition take
the place of fur, claws, tusks, and instincts in the quest for food
and shelter."

As Dr. Childe reviews the transition from the levels here described through cultures which employed metallurgy, commerce between distant parts, through the beginnings of the "industrial revolution," he summarizes the results of man's creativity in the following way (page 179):

"The economic revolution just described was possible only because the Sumeranians, Egyptians and Indians disposed of a body of accumulated experience and applied science. The revolution inaugurated a new method of transmitting experience, fresh ways of organizing knowledge, and more exact sciences. The science necessary for the revolution had been transmitted in the form of craft lore by oral precept and example. The beginnings of writing and of mathematics and the standardization of weights and measures coincide in time with the revolution. The synchronism is not accidental. The practical needs of the new economy had, in fact, evoked them."

84. Lloyd Morgan wrote a book called *Emergent Evolution*. It was published by Henry Holt in 1922. In it he writes of the process that he calls emergent evolution. On page 67 he says: "We must bear in mind that relatedness in the world at large, and in everything there in, is au fond fluent and ever changing.

"On this understanding, emergent evolution seeks to interpret, on the one hand, the persistence and continuity of natural event, and, on the other hand, progressive advance with novelty."

After summoning a vast array of scientific fact and logical deduction, he says, on page 281: "The question for us then arises: May we bring emergence itself under the rubric of causation? The reply turns on our answer to a further question: Is emergent evolution itself the expression of an orderly and progressive development? If so, (and such is my contention), then emergence itself takes rank, as Mills and Lewes also contended, among the 'laws of nature.' "

85. In an unpublished study of problem solving conducted by one of the authors at the University of Michigan, it became evident that the most efficient solver of problems was not necessarily the subject with the highest IQ or the highest rating in tests of manipulative ability. These were only crucial when the subject had the ability to let go of a wrong answer. The highest IQ

among the subjects tried the same wrong solution thirty-two times, and saying on that occasion, "I think I tried that before." The low intelligences often succeeded by their complete lack of attachment to a proposed solution. The record of these studies is available only in film, at the Educational Psychology Laboratory, University of Michigan, 1935.

86. See also Julian Huxley, *Philosophy In a World at War*, pages 160-161. The use of this term to describe the formulation of that which is new follows a physical analogy. Imagination, which lets us see form or plan where it has not yet taken form or shape is one of the greatest tools for human advancement. See discussion of Piaget's 17 standards of conception, *Psychological Abstracts*, April, 1951.

87. Hadley Cantril, *The Why of Man's Experience* (Macmillan, 1950), page 159: "The outstanding characteristic of man is his capacity to participate in the creation of emergent value attributes which enrich the quality of his experience. It is this characteristic of man which makes him 'human,' that provides what is common to all members of humanity, no matter how varied their individuality as genetically patterned. It is because of this characteristic that both the individual and the species appear to follow an ever ascending path."

88. When vision begins to be translated into the real and the actual, comes into being, words fail for stating the facts. It approaches what Korzybski calls the unspeakable. Anna Hampstead Branch in *The Monk in the Kitchen* comes close: "And lo, what was not, is."

89. Sinnott, *Cell and Psyche*, page 109: "But if we can set up these problems against the background of life itself, if we can show that mind and body, spirit and matter are held together in equal as parts of that organized system which life is. . . .

"If each of us is thus an organized and organizing center, pulling in matter and energy and knitting them into precise patterns; and if we are able though in a small degree to create new patterns never known before, does this not suggest that we may actually be a part of the great creative power in nature and hold communion with it?"

90. Hadley Cantril, *The Why of Man's Experience*, page 160: "Man is a contributing party to his own action and in this sense

has free will. A whole host of both natural and social scientists now agree that man's actions are not rigidly determined either biologically or culturally. Man's freedom of choice has increased to such a degree of responsibility as a co-product of this freedom."

91. Sinnott, *Cell and Psyche*, page 88: "The purpose and the purposer are one. It is we who will do, not some foreign agent."

92. See Robert Louis Stevenson, *The House of Eld*, in *Fables*. Here after many adventures in many lands to discover why it was necessary to wear a gyve on the right leg. It made ulcers, which were painful. It hampered movement. When Jack returned, having paid painfully for his search, having killed his uncle and smitten his mother, he brought back the assurance that it was not necessary to wear it on the right leg. The really proper place was on the left leg.

93. It is important to note the derivation of the word "mistake." Our common pronunciation would lead us to think that it was some unusual sort of stake. On the contrary, we see it to be merely a mis-take. In all cases of mis-take the part of common sense seems to be to lay down the mis-taken and take again.

94. One author's experience in teaching averages in a fifth grade arithmetic is a case in point. The problem was to determine the average rate of travel. It stated that a man walked so many miles per hour. A boy on a bicycle at another rate, a horse and rider at another, and finally a train at still another. When at last the child had dutifully added and divided, he remarked in an injured tone, "But, gosh, there ain't nothing going at that gait when you get it."

The *Ladies' Home Journal* years ago ran a story of the boy who wrestled with a problem in fractions. This had to do with a deer which had been killed by a lion who ate a third of his kill. A wolf came on and ate a sixth of what was left. Next came a jackal, who ate one-quarter of what remained. Then the fox, the weasel each his fractional part. When the boy was brought to tears in his attempt to solve it, mother took a hand. She, too, "got nervous" when the fractions tangled her up. Dad then put down his paper, and began. After reading the problem and making a few desperate stabs at it, he threw book, papers and all, in the fire, settling it all quite simply with the unquestionable truth that "There wasn't no sense to it. After the jackal had been there, no other animal would touch it."

95. Hadley Cantril, *The Why of Man's Experience,* page 59: "Each transaction of living involves numerous capacities and aspects of man's nature which operate together. Each occasion of life can occur only through an environment, is imbued with some purpose, requires action of some kind and the reiteration of the consequences of action. Every action is based on some awareness or perception which in turn is determined by the assumptions brought to the occasion. These assumptions are in turn determined by past experience. All of these processes are interdependent."

Page 62: "The quality of experience will be related closely to the inclusiveness of factors taken into account. Inclusiveness means making more order out of less order by including more and more. By increasing the inclusiveness of the factors taken into account, we extend the range of the setting in which we can act with some degree of surety. But as the range of our milieu is extended, we apparently decrease the chances that our action will fulfill our hopes. For example, reflex activity takes place within a very narrow setting but has a very high reliability; habits occur in a somewhat larger setting and have a somewhat lower chance of being right; value judgments give the largest setting for effective action and are the most reliable guides for meeting new situations, but their reliability is low compared to reflexes or habits and they are therefore often tinged with anxiety."

96. Angyal, *Foundations for a Science of Personality,* pages 124-167: In his chapter on Biospheric Dynamics, Angyal discusses the weight that is attached to items of experience from externality. The terms of classification include advantage, disadvantage, irrelevance to personality purposes.

97. The driver of a car in modern traffic recognizes this necessity. The perception of what proves to be a large piece of building paper rolling across the street is first assessed to be, from its movement, a living thing, for which the vehicle we command may spell injury or death. The recognition of this possibility is at least as rapid as the increase in heart rate, and glandular adjustment of the muscle to calamity.

98. See Hoskins, *The Tides of Life.*

99. See Flanders Dunbar, *Emotions and Bodily Change.* Columbia University Press, 1935.

100. V. Gordon Childe, *What Happened in History*, pages 130-150: The author traces the additions to human equipment from earliest known facts in medieval times in Europe. Here one sees almost graphically how item after item rose to usage, served better the purposes of the people and thus brought in new eras.

101. John Dewey and Arthur F. Bentley wrote *Knowing and the Known*, published by the Beacon Press in 1949. In it they state: "From birth to death every human being is a PARTY so that neither he nor anything done or suffered can possibly be understood when it is separated from the fact of participation in an extensive body of transaction—to which a human being may contribute and which he modifies, but only in virtue of being a partaker in them."

102. Earl C. Kelley, *Education for What Is Real*, page 92: "The salient points of a school would then be: (1) we would try to ride with rather than against the tide of purpose; (2) we would start with children at a much younger age; (3) we would start with the concrete and let needed abstractions come from them; (4) we would keep knowledge in wholes; (5) we would work to develop a sense of surety; (6) we would use the community as an educational force and device; (7) we would use both rural and urban settings; (8) we would emphasize planning and cooperation as essential parts of personal or group problem solving; (9) we would cherish the value of failure and contriving."

103. Marie I. Rasey, *Something to Go By* (privately published, 1948): A twelfth grade class in world history became concerned with what would have to be considered when the diplomats went at the task of writing a peace treaty. At the suggestion of the teacher that it was probably a lot harder to write a treaty than people generally realized, these young people sold themselves the idea of trying. Individuals soon became partisans for the countries whose problems they studied. When the semester ended with the treaty still unwritten, the young people had learned a vast array of factual matter concerning the history and economy of the various countries; they had acquired a great number of intense attitudes toward those often called foreigners; they were alert to the news as the papers recorded it. In short, they had acquired a fine store of attitudes, skills, and knowledge in the area of foreign

affairs. It would still be likely that an evaluation which was based on matching dates and battles might have found them wanting. One is inclined, however, to reverse the metaphor: one does not harvest thistles where fig trees have been planted.

104. Not only is it impossible to give a horse medicine democratically, one must also plant his crops before he harvests them, and one cannot express originality in the use of the telephone and expect to get the right number.

105. Du Nouÿ, *Human Destiny*, page 158: "All the ancestors of man were but irresponsible actors playing an imposed part in a play which they did not understand, or try to understand. Man continues to play his part but wants to comprehend the play. He becomes capable of perfecting himself, and he is even the only one capable of doing this. But in order to perfect himself he must be free, *since his contribution to evolution will depend upon the use he makes of his liberty.*"

106. A. N. Whitehead, *The Aims of Education*, page 18: "The mind is never passive: it is a perpetual activity, delicate, receptive, responsive to stimulus. You cannot postpone its life until you have sharpened it. Whatever interest attaches to your subject matter must be evoked here and now; whatever powers you are strengthening in the pupil must be exercised here and now; whatever possibilities of mental life your teaching should impart, must be exhibited here and now. That is the golden rule of education, and a very difficult one to follow."

107. A. N. Whitehead, *The Aims of Education*, page 63: "Mere passive observation is not sufficient. In creation only is there vivid insight into the properties of the object thereby produced. If you want to understand anything, make it yourself is a sound rule. Your faculties will be alive, your thoughts gain vividness by an immediate translation into acts. Your ideas gain that reality which comes from seeing the limits of their application."

108. It becomes obvious that the small group permits a closer relationship than is possible in an ordinary size class. Recognizing the uniqueness of each, it becomes simpler to share those commonalties, and fuse the differences when there are relatively few persons concerned.

109. For details of practice with small groups, see Earl C.

Kelley, *The Workshop Way of Learning*, Harper & Brothers, 1951.

110. Teacher-pupil planning which sounds so strange to some ears amounts primarily to consultation about what is to be done, how it shall be planned and carried out and appraised. It can be begun with no greater innovation than to substitute for the statement "Now we are going to" a simple question: "What do you think we should do first?" If this question can be sincerely asked, the rest follows.

111. H. S. Elliott wrote a book called *Group Thinking*. It was published by Association Press in 1928. On page 72 he says: "If he [the leader] acts as if he were the referee for a fight, then he will have the spirit of a fight. If he pits one side against another in order to make the discussion lively, he will have a contest on his hands. If he tries to turn the discussion toward a point of view with which he agrees, and does not give other points of view a chance, he will develop resentment and bad feeling. . . . The safeguard of fairness comes in the chairman's trust of the group process."

112. Research goes on in this area but the problem presents difficulties which have not so far been settled. The research needs to be small enough that each will find it easy to speak and be heard. It must be large enough so that the entity that comes to be established is greater in its totality than the mere summation of its respective members would be, for that totality which emerges as the group fuses, produces fresh power to find solutions. Experience indicates that a group can be too small as well as too large for best results.

113. Those who lack skill in the field of teaching and are therefore insecure when they find themselves in a position of teacher in a group, are likely, out of their anxiety, to undertake to be dictatorial. They mistake tasks which are tedious for tasks which are hard. They talk about making the learners sweat without realizing that they mix their figures.

114. All the pronoun we need is "we." "I have discovered the real meaning of pronouns. I did not learn it from my grammar either, 'They' in the sentence "They ought to do something about it," merely means we ought to, before the persons concerned are quite ready to accept their social responsibility. I is usually ob-

jectionable, and most often inaccurate, for there are few things indeed which I can do without the help of others. You puts distance between me and the others, like looking through a telescope wrong end to. Finally, we is all we need." Student comment.

115. Julian Huxley, *The Uniqueness of Man,* page 21: "Man represents the culmination of that process of organic evolution which has been proceeding on this planet for over a thousand million years. That process, however wasteful and cruel it may be, and into however many blind alleys it may have been diverted, is also in one respect progressive. Man has now become the sole representative of life in that progressive aspect and its sole trustee for any progress in the future."

116. Huxley again, page 28: "To put the matter in another way, progress has hitherto been a rare and fitful product of evolution. Man has the possibility of making it the main feature of his own future evolution, and of guiding its course in relation to a deliberate aim."

117. Karen Horney, *Neurosis and Human Growth,* page 377: "However great man's possibility for becoming destructive, the history of mankind also shows an alive and untiring striving toward greater knowledge about himself and the world around him, toward deeper religious experiences, toward greater achievements in all fields, and toward better ways of life. And his very best energies go into these strivings."

118. Karl T. Compton: Special interview: "It is always the optimists, albeit guided by knowledge and sensible caution, who get things done."

119. L. L. Whyte, *The Unitary Process in Physics and Biology,* page 14: "The unitary principle is simple but as yet unfamiliar. To minds accustomed to conceptions of permanence it must appear strange, for it selects as the invariant in change a persisting tendency."

Page 42: "The scientist may be a philosophical dualist or pluralist, but as a scientist he must seek to discover the relation between these two sides of approach so as to establish a single order in knowledge. When the relation of mental to material causality is understood, he will not longer be confronted with the false choice of interpreting the totality as either mental or material. For on the unitary view there is one universal formative process; matter, energy, life, and mind, are names which man has given to different aspects of that universal process. There is process; but there is no essence, no subtance, and no static existence."

120. A. N. Whitehead wrote *Science and The Modern World*. It was published by Macmillan in 1925. On page 206 he says: "The trees in Brazilian forests depend upon the association of various species of organisms, each of which is mutually dependent on the other species. A single tree by itself is dependent upon all the adverse chances of shifting circumstances. The wind stunts it; the rain denudes its soil; its leaves are blown away and are lost for the purpose of fertilization . . . But in nature the normal way in which trees flourish is by their association in a forest."

121. Page 207: "In fact, nature began by producing animals incased in hard shells for the defense against the ills of life. It also experimented with size. But smaller animals, without external armor, warm-blooded, sensitive, and alert have cleared these monsters off the face of the earth. Also, the lions and tigers are not the successful species. There is something in the ready use of force which defeats its own object. Its main defect is that it bars co-operation. Every organism requires an environment of friends, partly to shield it from violent changes, and partly to supply it with its wants."

122. John Dewey says, in correspondence with us: "The point I have in mind may be indicated best perhaps by your phrase *if* an individual needs others. I can't see any if about it. One's needs of others are plain necessities. Connection of need and necessity is more than etymological. The human being is born a helpless infant and in many cases he can't even start breathing without a friendly smack. He certainly needs others for supplying food and drink without which even physical existence wouldn't occur."

123. L. L. Whyte, *Everyman Looks Forward*, page 20: "Frustration is perpetual and inevitable but its damaging effects are overcome if a formative process remains dominant . . . All aggression is due to frustration and fear, but frustration does not necessarily lead to aggression."

124. It is not accurate to say that religion, or democracy, or any other ism has failed until we are sure that it has been tried.

A project may turn out badly for either of two causes: the facts may be false; the method of their application may be wrong. Twenty-five years ago an English teacher who was a senior adviser paid me a visit. She came, she said, to tell me what a fine "project" she had going. "My Seniors have planned to give a Shakespeare play for their class play." My comment was that that must have required some doing, since young folks, at that age, had quite other ideas of what was funny. "Yes," she answered, "it was hard. At first they wanted to do 'Was it Murder?' But I said, Shakespeare or nothing, so they chose Shakespeare."

125. Du Nouÿ, *Human Destiny*, page 130: "Today things have changed. We can conceive a harmonious cosmos the laws of which reenforce religious aspirations without ever contradicting them."

Page 107: "We started rationally from the critical study of evolution and were driven to admit the criterion of liberty, the freedom of choice, implying conscience and the sense of human dignity. The idea of God emerged progressively as an absolute necessity."

126. Sinnott, *Cell and Psyche*, page 111: "As James once said, we may come to recognize that this higher part of us is continuous with a *more* of the same quality operative in the universe outside and with which we can keep in working touch.

"Does this not indeed present as clear a picture as the scientist can draw of God Himself and our relation to Him?"

127. Albert Einstein, *The World As I See It:* "The state of mind which enables a man to do work of this kind [physics] is akin to that of the religious worshipper or the lover; the daily effort comes from no deliberate intention of program, but straight from the heart." Quoted by Howey, in supplement to the *American Weekly,* 1948, called *Faith of Men of Science*, page 4.

The words "love" and "charity" have been referred to from time to time through this text. Cooperation, which has inherent in it the concepts of the golden rule, and religion as defined by James in the New Testament. The loving of one's neighbor becomes an efficient way of life, and a sociological necessity. These can be multiplied many times if we make selection from all religions.

128. Karen Horney, *Neurosis and Human Growth*, page 197: In speaking of the arrogant-vindictive type, she says: "Great writers have intuitively grasped this pattern and have presented them (in

fiction) in more impressive form than a psychiatrist can hope to do. I am thinking of Captain Ahab, in *Moby Dick,* of Heathcliff in *Wuthering Heights,* and of Julian in *The Red and the Black.*"

In describing these people, she says (page 199): "He is convinced that everybody at bottom is malevolent and crooked, that friendly gestures are hypocritical, that it is only wisdom to regard everyone with distrust unless he has been proved honest. But even such proof will readily make room for suspicion at the slightest provocation. In his behavior toward others he is openly arrogant, often rude and offensive, although this is sometimes covered over by a thin veneer of civil politeness. In subtle and gross ways, with or without realizing it, he humiliates others and exploits them.

"He is a past master in frustrating others—frustrating their small and big hopes, their need for attention, reassurance, time, company, enjoyment. When others remonstrate against such treatment, it is their neurotic sensitivity that makes them react this way."

129. Du Nouÿ has remarked: "Action follows conviction, not knowledge."

130. Norman Cousins, *Modern Man Is Obsolete,* pages 47-49: "So we return full circle to man himself, to the animal that must operate world government. Is he wise enough to use greater power for greater good? Is he wise enough to create a common sovereignty and yet keep the ultimate power in his own hands?

"This is the multiple nature of the challenge to modern man— to bring about world government and to keep it pure; to keep his social, economic, and political institutions apace with his scientific achievements; to make whatever adjustments are required in his own make-up, conditioning, and outlook on life to exist in an Atomic Age.

"And if we reject the multiple challenge before us? And if we decide that we are not yet ready for world governmnt? What then? Then there is an alternative . . . Let him systematically abolish science and the tools of science. Let him destroy all machines and the knowledge which can build or operate those machines. Let him raze his cities, smash his laboratories, dismantle his factories, tear down his universities and schools, burn his libraries, rip apart his art. Let him murder his scientists, his lawmakers, his statesmen, his doctors, his teachers, his mechanics, his merchants, and anyone who has anything to do with the machinery of knowledge and progress. Let him punish literacy with death. Let him eradicate nations and set up the tribe as sovereign. Let him, in short, revert to his condition in society in 10,000 B.C. Thus emancipated from science, from progress, from government, from knowledge, from thought, he can be reasonably certain of prolonging his existence on this planet. This can be a way out—if 'modern man' is looking for a way out from the modern world."

131. Frank Townsend has written a long poem called *Heaven*. It was published by Knopf in 1930. He ends the poem with these lines:

Suddenly there appeared once more to me
The same wise old man whom I had seen
    on Mount Meditation
He said:
A long way from here there is a garden
And in the garden lives a Being,
In whom are the faculties of Creation and Understanding,
    and of rhythm.

The story of my journey to that garden is written in
Astronomy and in geology,
And in the history of plants and of the animals and of
    the human race.
As to the garden,
Innumerable books have been written about it,
And about every part of it.

The Being who lives in the garden,
In whom are the faculties of Creation and Understanding
    and Rhythm,
Is Man.

INDEX

Date Due